Sorry,
I'm a fellow Shelton Gal —
all but recital and theater.

Louie

Watch for other titles from

Running Angel Books and

Louise Thomas

at

www.secondwindpublishing.com

Dear Emily: A Memoir

My Life in the Fine Stores

By
Louise Thomas

Running Angel Books
Published by Second Wind Publishing, LLC.
Kernersville

Running Angel Books
Second Wind Publishing, LLC
931-B South Main Street, Box 145
Kernersville, NC 27284

First Running Angel Books edition published April 2011.
Running Angel Books, Running Angel logo, and all
production design are trademarks of Second Wind
Publishing, used under license.

For information regarding bulk purchases of this book,
digital purchase and special discounts, please contact the
publisher at www.secondwindpublishing.com

Cover design and interior sketches by Gail Morris
Chanel purse icon courtesy of Susette L. Sides

Manufactured in the United States of America

ISBN 978-1-935171-53-9

Dedication:

To: Emily Lawrence who loved the fine stores as much as I

To: Marilyn Hartsell, Ellen Thomas

To: Pamela Holbrook, Gus Holbrook, Jennifer Holbrook Enger, Matthew Enger, Brayden Enger, Charles Thomas Hartsell, Paige Vaughn Hartsell, Alexander Kennedy Hartsell, Sara Grace Hartsell, Carolyn Elizabeth Hartsell and Augustus Maxwell Hartsell

To: Charles Thalhimer, Sherwood Michael, and Dick Ayscue

To: Evelyn Sosnik (deceased) and to all the buyers and supporting staff at the many Thalhimer stores

Finally, to all of the customers: Thank you for your years of loyalty. Without you, the fine stores would not have existed.

Table of Contents

Preface

Emily and I met the first year of my first job, and we have remained friends ever since. We lived in three East Coast cities simultaneously and corresponded faithfully in between. She found the fabulous department stores just as exciting as I did. She recalls when shopping was a fun and rewarding experience (as finding a wide assortment of shoes in size 8 1/2 AAAA on any shopping trip). What made the department store, an American institution that took decades to perfect, disappear so rapidly?

After more than thirty exciting years in retailing, I returned to my former Cape Cod shingle and faced the daunting task of reclaiming my much neglected, all but destroyed, perennial garden. Three years later, I traded my Cardiac Rehab program at Wake Forest University that was only minutes from my home, for a slot in the Liberal Arts M.A. program at the same University. The idea of pursuing subjects in depth that I had previously avoided, or that had not been available, appealed to me. The experience far exceeded my expectations. The professors were outstanding, and the small classes of mature students encouraged stimulating discussions. I had favorite classes. They were "German Literature from Medieval Days until World War II", "Ancient Japanese Literature through This Century", and "The Country House Movement in America". I was pleased when Mark Alan Hewitt, the author of our textbook for the last course, spoke at Reynolda House the following spring.

With only one three-hour course scheduled each semester, I soon started working on the thesis that the University had approved: "Greed, Gall, and Gaff, What

Happened to the Grand Emporiums". It is the social history of this country in the twentieth century, a reminder of the time when service, civility, and good taste were paramount. After I'd submitted fifteen queries, six editors agreed to read the manuscript. Comments were favorable, but each editor suggested that if I presented the work in first person, he would reconsider.

The bound 244-page thesis was put aside until friends convinced me that I had an interesting story, well worth rewriting. A friend who had had fifty refusals is now working on her second novel for a happy publisher.

Part One:

From Virginia to New York

"You'll find B. Altman over there, Madam, not far from Best & Company and Franklin Simon."

Chapter One

Our Meeting

Dear Emily,

Our paths have intertwined for years. Our interests, though wide, were never far apart. We often fail to complete a conversation. This will be my chance for the last word. A cold, confining winter seems a fitting time to reminisce and try to answer your questions about what happened to the grand old emporiums we were introduced to when we lived in New York City. To this day, we have not accepted the mundane life without them. With the arrival of spring, my mature garden will start unfolding daily and will steal much of my time if only to walk the stone paths in the woods and admire each peeping bulb. Snowdrops, aconites, wood hyacinth, grape hyacinth, bloodroot, trillium, hellebore, Jacob's Ladder, Virginia bluebell, followed by jonquils and beds of colorful primrose is a pallet that only nature can paint.

Although I cannot recall exactly how you and I met, I feel that we must have been introduced by your apartment mate, since she and I worked in the same building at NACA (now NASA), at Langley Field, in Tidewater, Virginia. Several months of practice

1

teaching had turned a would-be-teacher into a mathematician for engineers doing aeronautical research. Filled with ambition, I realized that I was not suited for a government job. Also my work was not that interesting. It seemed to me that those who only clocked in and out got the same salary increase as those who were dedicated. At the Flight Tunnel, some of the engineers projected the image of being more interested in the sailboats they were building after work and on weekends, than the project to which they were assigned. Did you work in the same building as Betty Anderson?

Your decision to move to New York and your glowing reports gave me the courage to follow. Two visits in the prior eighteen months had convinced me that it was the fashion hub. Thank you for a grand introduction.

Remember when 5th Avenue was the fashion street of the world! Paris, Rome, and London had been devastated by the war. Before World War II, all high fashion came from Europe. Couture buyers from the best stores made four crossings each year with steamer trunks in tow, and never missed an opening. After the War, smart merchants in New York encouraged promising young American designers to be more creative. Claire McCardell was the first American designer on the cover of "*Time*". She was a Parson graduate and was hailed as the launcher of American sportswear. Europe emerged from the war so battered that it was years before the high fashion lines were ready to entice foreign buyers. With the European market in limbo, Pauline Trigere and Norman Norell opened showrooms in New York; Charles James followed from London. Fashion offerings in the hinterland had never been so enticing.

How fortunate we were to be able to browse and,

funds permitting, make an occasional purchase at
Bergdorf Goodman, Bonwit Teller, The Tailored
Woman (known for its wide assortment of coats),
DePinna, I. Miller, and Saks (the salesgirls were
fashion plates). Past 42nd Street and the library was my
favorite store—Lord & Taylor, under the leadership of
Dorothy Shaver. Continuing across 38th Street was
Sloan's with its exciting room vignettes. "*House and
Gardens*" had failed to prepare me for the handsome
antiques and exciting accessories. Moving down the
avenue, one reached Best, the children's store, and
McCuchen's, the fine fabrics linens store. Russek's was
to suits, what Tailored Woman was to coats. Across the
street and filling an entire block stood the venerable B.
Altman where the profits went to New York City
charities. The first floor, with its extremely wide aisles
and handsome rich wooden display cases, was designed
to accommodate the "carriage trade". In B. Altman's
early days, the downtown customers had to shop from
their carriages during the winter months, because the
streets were unpaved and walking into the store was
prohibitive.

Only two fine fashion stores have survived—
Bergdorf Goodman and Saks. Lord & Taylor remains in
name only. The May Company lacks experience in
operating a fine store. Bloomingdale's is far removed
from the pacesetting days of Marvin Traud, under
whom the Home Store vignettes attracted
unprecedented crowds. Minus the handsome fabrics and
superb tailoring, Bloomingdale's clothes are now more
trendy than fashionable.

Often I regret that I gave most of my designer
clothes to the North Carolina History Museum for I am
still the same size. After shopping for hours, I usually
come home and appreciate a Gloria Sachs, a Bill Blass,

3

or an Ellen Tracy more than when it was purchased. With fabric the first component of any garment, there is little hope for improvement in what's being offered in fashion today.

Love,

Laurie

Chapter Two

My Early Days

Dear Emily,

You and I are each from small North Carolina towns, but their similarities end there. Murfreesboro is located between the Roanoke and Chowan rivers in the northeastern part of the state and conducted trade with Virginia and England. Your ancestors were English, both maternal and paternal. Due to trade relations with New England, many of the early buildings reflect New England architecture. There were comfortable private residences as well as plantations. Soon, the progressive settlement had two newspapers and two better female colleges. Today, it is a beautifully restored eighteenth and nineteenth century jewel consisting of a twelve-block historical district plus other related areas and the Mulberry Grove Plantation. There is the home of John Hall Wheeler, first president of the Charlotte Mint, the home of Dr. Robert Gatling, inventor of the famed Gatling gun, and the home of Dr. Walter Reed. I was greatly impressed the time I was there and much has been done since. You have every reason to be proud of your progressive hometown.

In stark contrast, I was born in Stanley County, the

"back country". Historians gave the designation to that part of our new country, which was settled primarily by Germans who traveled down the valleys from Pennsylvania, Virginia, and North Carolina in search of rich soil and water. The discovery of gold, the first in the new country, was also an attraction. My Thomas ancestors came from Kent, England early in the 1700s, settled in Kent County, Maryland, and Kent County, Virginia before claiming a land grant in Anson County, North Carolina. Through gifts of land, my grandfather and father settled in Stanley County, an area that was primarily rural until the Southern Railway decided in 1913 to build a depot to serve the cotton and grain farmers. It was the first small town to develop aside from the county seat, Albemarle, seven miles away. It was a thriving small town until the new 27/29 highway connecting Charlotte (twenty plus miles west) and Raleigh (the Capital) bypassed our village. The depot has been handsomely restored and landscaped. The rumor is that a commuter train will run from Charlotte to relieve the highways of the heavy traffic. The village is eventually destined to become a bedroom of Charlotte—good for business but bad for the environment.

In the early 2000s, the University of North Carolina, Chapel Hill, conducted a dig on a nearby river. The Oakboro Historical Museum has a credible collection of Indian artifacts dating to 10,000 B.C. When Alcoa excavated for its dam, hundreds of thousands of Indian artifacts were bulldozed making our state the site of more old Indian artifacts than any state east of the Mississippi.

Until recently, I assumed nothing interesting had happened to me until after college and my first job. In the summer of 2005, my niece and I spent a day visiting childhood sites and reminiscing. After a sportswear manufacturing plant closed and left 600 people unemployed, many were ready to write off the village of 1500 people. Instead, we found it robust and thriving. My priority was to deliver some pictures of my father to the five-year-old regional museum in the small village where I spent my first fifteen years. The bright, energetic and dedicated volunteer curator was so happy to discover a "live one" from the collection era that she insisted that I put on paper anything of interest I could recall.

My childhood days might not have been the most exciting, but I shall always be indebted to my parents for their constructive influence on my formative years. Salt of the earth, they instilled in their children integrity, respect, hard work, and confidence that they could attain any goal they wished. Church and education were priorities at our house. Although not the most demonstrative, my parents loved their four children dearly as attested by their unselfish sacrifice. We sometimes questioned their frugality, but how else could they have sent four children to college during the Depression?

My father attended Rutherford College and taught for a few years after he was married at age twenty-six. He had a quick mind. Math was his strong suit, and he often helped me with my lessons. Mother attended the Palmerville Academy, but admitted that she was not a very good student. She preferred gardening, cooking, sewing, and caring for her house and family. Her love for gardening made a lasting impression on me.

Born on March 14, 1922 to Millard Winston Thomas and Jennie Smith Thomas, I was fortunate enough to join two older brothers, Harvey Lee, seven, and Robert Brady, five. My earliest recollection was crawling across a wide pine floor on a porch to claim a huge doll my parents were offering me. It was a happy time.

The next vivid picture was riding in our Model T Ford when I was likely about two. (Babies were kept home to avoid germs.) Autos were a status symbol then just like today. When I was four, we traded up to a Chevrolet—no more make do—with windows to take down in the spring and re-hang in the fall. While visiting a playmate, Grant's mother asked him to share a bowl of apples with me. His agitated response was, "No! Louise has a new car. I don't!"

Unusually kind to me, my siblings taught me how to climb but failed to teach me how to get down. When learning to ride their bike, I consistently managed to hit the obstruction they warned me to avoid. Any wonder I was not invited to play baseball or basketball with the neighborhood teams? Since there were few girls in our neighborhood, books became my best friends. Occasionally there would be enough people to select actors and have others to make up an audience. We would hang sheets at the top of the stairs, used as seats. Those afternoons time stood still. Our models were the few traveling professional shows that came to our school once or twice a year.

After having two sons, my mother was delighted to have a daughter to dress. My earliest clothes were heavily smocked cotton print and silk dresses with matching smock-trimmed pantaloons. My favorites were a natural silk pongee (with raw silk slubs) and a weighted smooth pink silk. (My Aunt Bessie bought the fabric on one of her trips). Each had beautifully smocked yokes, sleeves, and pantaloons. Our neighbor commented that with silks on a four-year-old, only

Paris would be good enough when she grew up.

My mother's colorful flower garden was the prettiest I had seen and by far the show place of the neighborhood. In front of the back fence that enclosed the vegetable garden, were clumps of jonquil and wood hyacinth. Later in the season, hollyhock and larkspur formed a backdrop. The large rectangular shaped garden was to the right side of the house and included an orchard of apple and pear trees near the back. As a border, she planted flowering shrubs of forsythia, pink almond, flowering quince, spireas, and weigela.

A riot of color claimed the remaining space. There were many more annuals than perennials because the latter had not been highly developed then. Sweet peas were so bountiful they required staking and tying. Luscious nasturtiums spilled over the well-manicured soil. More larkspur, abundant cosmos, dahlias, huge pompon mums (staked), zinnias, snow-on-the-mountain, touch-me-nots, dusty miller, sunflowers, gladiolus, and bearded iris are some I remember. Many of these are seldom seen today. I do not recall ever spraying or dusting for insects.

Her love of flowers went beyond growing them. She loved to bring them into the house and also to share them. Often she would furnish flowers for church. Two arrangements I remember were white Annabel hydrangea, pierced by spikes of purple butterfly bush, and the other, impressive giant gold mums interspersed with ruffled pink kale. They would be impressive today. My sister does great arrangements; I enjoy trying. We each have been dedicated gardeners.

I must have been between three and four when my mother had a goiter operation in a Charlotte hospital. She got along fine, and the next day my father took me with him for a hospital visit. It was my first trip to

Charlotte and I was impressed by a talking parrot in the hospital lobby. "Polly wants a cracker," was its complete repertoire. Daddy and Aunt Bessie brought Mother home several days later. Aunt Corrine relieved Aunt Bessie, as bed rest would probably last a week or more.

Our father taught for six to eight years in three schools that we can identify in the area of Oakboro: Barbee's Grove, Hatley's Grove, and Mineral Springs. In each instance, they were sited near a church of the same name. Maybe this assured the students of a passable road at all times of the year. Usually, one room meant one teacher. We have a photograph of Father and sixty-two students at Barbee's Grove, ages five to twenty-six. Teaching the three R's to this many pupils was possible only because the small children were taught respect by their parents, and the older students (many older than the teacher) felt fortunate to have the opportunity to learn. Some aspired to own a business; others wanted to become successful farmers. Discipline was never a problem.

There were more small wooden school buildings scattered through the sparsely settled countryside than there were qualified teachers, which meant that the teachers went to the schools that served the most pupils. Aunt Bessie lived with our parents the second year of their marriage and taught at Mineral Springs, about four miles away. They either rode horseback or hitched up a buggy.

Dad took great pride in his teaching, and I have been told that he was a good teacher. He taught the Palmer writing method. This was the last era of beautiful handwriting. Happy in a profession that made a contribution to the community, he would have remained a teacher if granddaddy Thomas hadn't reminded him that he could not support a family on a teacher's salary. Granddaddy had been given a sizable farm by his wife's father when he married and decided to gift his first son, my father, a farm. Granddaddy Smith met the occasion by giving them money to build a comfortable eight-room house with lots of porches and fireplaces.

When my father helped me with my lessons, he sometimes talked about his teaching experiences. One is still a vivid picture. For more than a year, he shared a two-room school with a neighbor of ours, Mr. Harris. His strongest qualification was that he and his six children were all talented, self-taught musicians. One son supposedly played the violin for the Philadelphia Symphony Orchestra under the baton of maestro Eugene Ormandy. My father had a disciplined mind and was dedicated to preparing his students as well as he could in the allotted time. His co-teacher was assigned to the first through fifth grades but spent more time teaching music than preparing them in the basic reading, writing, and arithmetic. Every time a plane passed over, his students stormed out to see it. Afterwards, they would noisily charge back in and spend the rest of the day entertaining the class with their imaginary trip on the one-engine plane. My father thought it a waste of time as many parents sacrificed to send their children to school. It was also disruptive to his students. Today, it would be considered progressive teaching.

I spent many a balmy afternoon under a Chinaberry tree watching the planes fly over and imagining myself in Paris, Rome, London, and Tokyo. (My favorite doll was a Japanese beauty with her parasol.) Dreaming was sufficient. I never expected to get nearer to Paris than my front yard.

Our place was idyllic to a six-year-old with a curious mind. Not far from the back yard was a clear flowing stream with plenty of large stones to hop and smaller ones to overturn, exposing fish, tadpoles, crawfish, frogs and turtles. Beyond the stream rose the tallest hill in the neighborhood. On snowy days, which I remember as being often, all the neighborhood boys arrived early and built a large bonfire at the peak. Sometimes my brothers would let me ride with them if I would help pull the sled back to the top. Sledders had so much speed that occasionally they lost control and landed in the stream. Tired and happy snow warriors headed home for a hot meal by mid-afternoon. Ice froze over our pond but was seldom thick enough for skating.

One picture-perfect afternoon, my younger brother, Brady, and I were looking for four-leaved clovers in a meadow below the house, being careful to avoid the competing bees. The silence was interrupted only by birds rehearsing from a nearby locust tree. My brother decided to move on to something more challenging. I thought a bed of sweet-smelling clover was ideal for my afternoon nap. Unfortunately, my green print dress was a perfect disguise in the clover. About twenty minutes later, I was awakened by a large tractor wheel passing over my right mid arm. My screaming and waving of my left arm and struggling to rise were a signal to my older brother, Harvey, at the wheel. He managed to stop the monster just as the enormous cleats were within inches of my head. Harvey was more frightened than I was. The sinister scene was difficult for him to forget. Dad and Mother rushed me to the Albemarle Hospital where I was fitted with splints and plaster of Paris. Except for overnight stays with Granddaddy and Grandmother Smith and Aunt Bessie, I had spent no nights away from my family. In the late

1920s, a broken arm meant a five-night stay in the hospital. When asked why I refused my breakfast of orange juice, oatmeal, toast, jelly, and milk the next morning, I asked if that was all they had.

"We have this at home," I said, "I thought you would have something different."

Maybe I thought I was in a hotel.

After this near casualty, my brother Harvey became my devoted lifetime guardian. He escorted me to my classroom and saw that I was settled on my frightful first day of school. He saw that I found the right school bus. The second day, after recess, I decided to join him in the seventh grade. My teacher came for me and herded me back to my room while I sobbed and announced to anyone within earshot that I didn't like her. After a reprimand at home, my worst offense at school was talking too much, for which the punishment was standing in the corner.

How we loved visiting our Smith grandparents and Aunt Bessie every time the occasion arose. They lived about seven miles away in Locust. Granddaddy was an ambitious, over-achieving third generation German. A large landowner, he aimed to be self-supporting. Orchards, vineyards, an extensive vegetable garden, fowl, pork, and beef supported his plan. He was ahead of his time. Granddaddy owned the first tractor in the area and had the first generator-operated electrical system. His big, black Durant touring car and driver was his indulgence.

Apples, pears, cantaloupe and watermelon were wrapped in newspaper and stored along with root vegetables in a root cellar under my grandparent's house. The wrapped fruits, melons, and nuts were brought out on our visits. Ice was cut and stored in sawdust in the winter for summer ice cream. Aunt

Bessie taught the first grade and had more books than anyone I knew. Mother said that my curiosity and love of travel came from her because of those books.

I was enchanted with Granddaddy's collection of gold coins. Nights when the grownups were visiting, he would go to his safe in a walk-in closet and get a tobacco pouch of coins for me to stack and count. Mother feared I would lose one. She always felt that he buried some of them rather than turn them in when all gold was called by the U. S. government in 1931.

We felt that his affection for gold was flamed by the fact that he owned land near, if not adjacent to, the farm where the first gold was discovered in America. In 1779, a twelve-year-old boy found a seventeen pound gold rock in Little Meadow creek in Cabarrus County. By 1825, there were nearly 100 gold mines in a twenty-mile radius of Charlotte, then a "boomtown". The U. S. Mint opened a branch in 1837 in a hamlet that was remembered as Indian trading paths. Granddaddy was born at mid-century and was influenced by a gold-driven economy. He always expected to find gold in a nearby creek that ran through his farm. Uncle E. B. inherited the farm and the same high expectations of finding the "big one". Charlotte became the big winner. Unlike Richmond and Charleston, Charlotte had no past, only a highly enviable future triggered by the accidental discovery of a rare mineral in another county.

Granddaddy Smith died in 1930 when I was eight. I was crushed. It marked the end of our backyard summer reunions with uncles, aunts and cousins. Afterwards, Christmas never included everyone. The money was divided equally with no complaints; the land division was not so easy. The land was surveyed, appraised and sized into ten parcels. We never understood why

Granddaddy left his wife only a child's portion unless it was because she and Aunt Bessie had insurance policies from the two sons who died in the flu epidemic during World War I. Grandmother and three children highly disapproved. Three siblings accepted. Three attempted to remain neutral. All the cousins suffered, because holidays were never the same. An annual reunion for the last twenty years has filled the void.

In the spring of 1931, our bucolic life had a terrible reversal. Although we grew up during the lean years, our parents were responsible, and we were always confident there would be money for a college education. Each of us had bank savings equal to one or two years of college. Our grandparents gave us money at holidays that went into a college account. What had taken years to accumulate vanished one morning at the breakfast table when my father calmly announced that our local bank had closed. The banker and directors met the night before and agreed that the inspector, due on Friday, would not accept the audit. The Depression had been causing havoc for several years. Crops produced few clear dollars. Merchants sold on credit or didn't sell. Two merchant brothers were the bank's biggest debtors. They were also on the board of directors. My father and Mr. Teeter, directors, went home from the distressful Thursday night meeting. The Coble brothers, Jason and Guilford, went to their lawyer's home and deeded everything they owned to their wives, evading all responsibility. I can recall sitting in a car on Saturday afternoon in front of Furr's Café and watching customers cross the street rather than walk in front of the Coble store. News of their actions spread like wildfire. After a few months, the store closed while the Teeter store next door expanded.

Mother cried for a week. Father had invested her

recent inheritance in bank stock. Four accounts, plus lots of worthless stocks made us all but penniless. Mother had plans to treat herself to some luxuries. Instead, my parents had to raise money to redeem the stock at full price that was sold at auction at a discount. Sometime later, the depositors were issued cash for about twenty percent of their savings. My older brother had to delay his college education. When I read of all the lying, cheating and greed of our executives today, I feel only pride that my father was a man of integrity.

In the midst of this turmoil, my baby sister arrived. Although I was nine, I had no inkling we were expecting an addition. It was a fortunate distraction from all that had happened earlier. We now had the ideal family, two boys and two girls. By the time Marilyn started to school, I was headed for college, and two brothers were already in college. I have heard her say she thought all playmates were black until she started to school.

The choice of college was made for me. Mother had two first cousins on the staff at Mars Hill College; aunts and uncles had preceded me. Carolyn Biggers was Dean of Women, and her sister, Martha, Head of the Music Department. They had held similar positions at Meredith College until Carolyn was involved in a terrible train accident. I was sixteen and a child of the Depression, so Mars Hill proved to be a good choice. The professors were superior, and pre-med and ministerial students dominated the campus. After the first semester, I learned to study and to accept the rigid routine. Each year I worked. My freshmen year I worked for an English professor and sophomore year as a lab assistant.

Most of my peers were transferring to UNC Chapel Hill, and I was set on doing the same. My older brother

16

had graduated from NC State University while my younger brother was still there. Although I was accepted and had a roommate, my older brother insisted that I was too young and immature to face the drinking and smoking at "The Hill'. I went to East Carolina, kicking and screaming. As I look back, I regret not being more challenged, but I doubt that any other road would have led to the same destination.

Pearl Harbor changed the world on December 7, 1941, which was my junior year. It was difficult to concentrate when my brothers and all the males I knew were expected to be called into service any day. Uncertainty was all on which I could depend. Brady graduated from NC State University with the class of 1942 and joined the Army in October of that year. He applied to the Air Corps, as did most of his classmates, and was greatly disappointed when his medical exam showed he was colorblind. That early in the war, chances of survival for a pilot were slim. In the Army's 2nd Division, he was assigned to Africa, Sicily, and England en route to the continent where he was responsible for supplies for his unit from D-Day until he was captured in Germany and held as a POW before his release six weeks later. When conditions allowed, he kept a diary, but talking about his war experiences later was painful. Among his many awards was a badge with seven Bronze Stars and a District Unit Oak Leaf. We were so thankful that he was spared, as he had spent four years at risk. Many of his classmates were not so fortunate.

Harvey graduated from NC State University the year I enrolled at Mars Hill College. Since he was a teacher, he was deferred from the draft, but after one year he became restless and tried to volunteer for the Navy. Because he was six foot and four inches tall, he

17

was not eligible for either branch of service. Persistent, he was accepted by the Merchant Marines as a purser and assigned to the Pacific theater. While they were at sea, he contracted malaria. The supply of drugs had been depleted, so he didn't get the needed treatment.

Times were tumultuous. Love reached higher peaks, and sorrow hit lower lows. I lost my second mother on December 9, 1941. Aunt Bessie, who had no children of her own, never met a child she didn't love. Petite and pretty, she taught first grade at Stanfield before transferring to her hometown, Locust. With a zest for life, she loved teaching first year students because she felt she got them at a most impressionable age. Blessed with many friends, she was kind, thoughtful and generous. She loved good clothes, travel, flowers and all things beautiful. Attending summer school in Asheville was high on her agenda many summers. Once she took me to Asheville for a long weekend at the Battery Park Inn. (F. Scott Fitzgerald and Zelda were regular guests). All the shop owners knew the generous customer and pampered us.

Since all my mother's brothers and sisters had heart problems, no one was too concerned that Aunt Bessie was seeing her doctor about her symptoms, until she had a severe heart attack and died in the hospital several days later. I was unable to get transportation to the funeral, but I have always cherished the fond memories of our good times together. One Christmas, I recall she asked Harvey to drive her to deliver food, warm clothing, shoes, blankets, quilts and kerosene to students she knew were in need. A positive influence on the lives of hundreds of children, hers might have been the only love they knew. A joy to her peers, she had many beaux to the end of her fifty-one beautiful years.

My senior year was most unsettling. All the men

18

were shipping out. A friend sent me his wings from Elgin Field, Florida and invited me to his graduation, but I did not go.

Physiology 103 was a dreaded requirement. Many took it as early as possible so they could repeat. Some took it via mail from other schools. The professor graded on the scale; thirty to forty percent expected to fail. All questions on the final were essay. After a few minutes, many students folded and signed their papers and left. Because there were no answers to be found in a book, many were unnerved. It was difficult to believe, but my name was at the top of grade posting.

The last semester I skipped practice teaching in town and was sent to a remote rural village that had seen three English teachers earlier that year. I made and mailed lesson plans for each day. If I got one response per class, I did well. Fathers or brothers were always in the service. There was a lack of respect for the school, the teacher, and lack of discipline in the home. There was no choice but to live in a teacherage with six older teachers. With no transportation but a greyhound bus, I spent three miserable months in an intolerable situation learning nothing, but I did get a salary.

Meanwhile, my Granddaddy Thomas, who had spent the last ten years living with us, died on April 14, 1943, at age ninety-one. He was an adventurous soul. Having been given a large, rich river farm by his father-in-law, he took on the role of gentleman farmer, delegating the labor to his children or other help. Never having met a stranger, he spent his time managing his livery stable in Oakboro, where he leased horses and transportation vehicles. He knew he was a winner when he leased his best-in-house horse and buggy to the town's first doctor, Dr. Hartsell. I tend to believe he was a native son, but I am not quite sure. Adjacent to the stables, Grandaddy also bought and sold cotton. At age thirteen, he recalled sitting on a fence and watching the Rebels march by. How he longed to be older so he could join the excitement.

To me, his most fascinating adventure took place at age eighteen. Restless and hearing of homesteading in Texas, he hopped a freight train and went to West Texas, where he knew that others from his area had gone. He wasted no time in registering and laying out a generous claim. The deed, to become valid, required that a certain portion had to be under cultivation by a stipulated time. After a few weeks, he and his Indian friends had cleared the brush from a section, laid out fields, and made plans for where crops would be planted. A deal was made with the Chief that he would be in charge until the new landowner could go home, get affairs in order, and return. Every detail seemed to be covered. The new landowner was surprised the morning he went by for one last handshake and was told by the Chief that the only way he could proceed with the plans was by marrying his oldest daughter. Granddaddy had other plans and caught the freighter home, minus his Texas dreams. We can only wonder how many oil wells lay beneath his West Texas empire.

How he regretted not being around during the California Gold Rush. As a reminder, he always carried a 1949 gold piece in a small tin in his breast coat pocket. Too bad he didn't live in the day when world travel was easy.

Back on campus for the last two weeks of school, recruiting agents were numerous. Females were being interviewed for jobs formerly considered male domain. Punk and I accepted offers from NACA (now NASA) at Langley Field, in Hampton, Virginia. She was a math major. I had a math minor. We each were to become mathematicians reporting to aeronautical engineers. We were to report to work two weeks later.

Harvey drove down for graduation and helped pack my belongings for two weeks at home with my parents and sister. Two professors had approached me with offers for scholarships, one to Ohio State in Economics and the other to Vanderbilt in English or Library Science. Due to the times, graduate offerings were not top priorities. Supporting the cause was. As it was my first real job, the future was frightening, and I often wondered if anything I'd ever done, read or experienced had in any way prepared me for this time.

There are a few sounds, smells and experiences not previously mentioned that should not be omitted, such as Daddy revving up the car in the drive every Sunday morning. He taught the adult men's Sunday school class from my early remembrances until he became homebound.

Another memory was the smell of homemade yeast rolls most Thursdays when we left the school bus. The yeast came from fresh hops grown on a front porch trellis and had a taste that was not to be duplicated. Usually there would be hot sweet buns the next morning made from the same dough.

Thanksgiving dinner was at our house with Uncle E. B. Smith, Aunt Ollie, and their two children, Margaret and Brady. The men always went hunting, while the women prepared the spread. The rich noodles Aunt Ollie made and brought were actually fettuccine, which I didn't know until years later and was not able to fully enjoy then because I was counting cholesterol. Mother always made Uncle E. B.'s favorite caramel cake as only she could. You could count on good food any time the Smiths met. The wives of the sons must have been good cooks to qualify. Uncle E. B. was the male version of Aunt Bessie. He was loving, caring, thoughtful, and happy. He was a bearer of gifts. He never met a stranger. He lost his business during the Depression, because he couldn't say "no" to his customers who forgot him when prosperity returned. He never found the large gold nugget, but he found hundreds of friends.

Daddy was a whiz with figures. He was the treasurer of his church, bank director, chairman of the new Church building committee, the PTA, his lodge and made many calculations for the neighbors. People building a house, barn or garage would bring their dimensions to him and he would itemize the needed lumber and supplies and give them the total cost. He calculated the interest on their anticipated loan. Many sought his advice on financial matters.

Harvey inherited the same affinity for figures. At his high school graduation, he was awarded a gold coin for outstanding math student. Had he lived, he would have been a successful businessman. I watched Dad add columns of six-digit numbers in no time. When I worked, I could add a long column much quicker than the time needed to transfer the numbers to a calculator. After years of experience, I could review a new line of clothing and be able to tell the buyer how much it would cost to put it into eight, eighteen, or twenty-six stores. There were A, B, and C stores with a percent allocated to each, which took out most of the room for error.

Although my father was seventh generation here, he and his father quoted so many of their childhood adages; one could have thought they had just walked down the gangplank. I can remember some:

Good fences make good neighbors.

Never hang your dirty wash on the line.

Beauty is as beauty does.

Early to bed and early to rise makes a man healthy, wealthy and wise.

The early bird gets the worm.

Birds of a feather flock together.

A stitch in time saves nine.

A penny saved is a penny earned.

Remember when you make your bed; you have to sleep in it.

Beauty is more than skin deep.

An apple doesn't fall far from the tree.

Clothes don't make the man.

Actions speak louder than words.

Right will win out.

Neither a lender nor a borrower be.

The easiest way to lose a friend, lend him money.

Never look a gift horse in the mouth.

Blood is thicker than water.

You can tell a person by the company he keeps.

Never put more on your plate than you can eat.

There's no friend like an old friend.

There are other ways to kill a cat than choking it on butter.

Never put off until tomorrow what you can do today.

Pride comes before the fall.

You have to face yourself in the mirror each morning.

Anything worth doing is worth doing well.

Emily, did you hear these saying at your home as well?

Love,

Laurie

Chapter Three

New York City

 Dear Emily,

With $900 from the sale of E bonds, supplemented by a meager checking account, I arrived at Penn Station as a frightened young Southern girl. After a few nights at the Barbizon for Women, on the East Side, I realized that my small savings would not last long and moved to the West Side, where I didn't feel safe. Emily, I have you to thank for finding me a place in your building on Morningside Drive, just two blocks from Riverside Drive and convenient to Columbia University, Grant's Tomb, and the magnificent Riverside Church. Amsterdam Avenue provided grocers, cleaners, pharmacy, stationers, as well as transportation.

On my first job, I modeled hats for a custom milliner, Mary Goodfellow, located on East 55th Street, just off Madison Avenue. Ms. Goodfellow had moved from Canada in search of a more lucrative market for her custom-made millinery. She was a talented designer with a successful business of referred customers who expected to pay from $100 to $500 for an original creation. In the late 1940s, walk-in customers did not spend that kind of money. Eleanor Lambeth, fashion editor for "*The New York Times*", brought in a well-worn nutria coat and wished to have a glamorous hat made. Ms Goodfellow graciously complied.

We were surprised when an unknown Mrs. Nichols walked in one afternoon and after a few minutes ordered three chapeaux for more than $600. When told that they would be ready in three to four weeks, she exclaimed that in three to four weeks she was apt to forget that she had ordered them and go out and order others. After some discussion, she agreed to wait. The transaction would not have been memorable had her husband's picture not appeared on the cover of the "*Daily Mirror*" the following weekend. Dressed in sailing attire and posing on the deck of a sixty-foot yacht anchored on Long Island Sound, Mr. Nichols' picture carried the headlines: "Banker Swindles $675,000 from Long Island Bank". Today the same story might be lost on page ten, but at that time, it was indeed big news and a rarity. Luckily, Ms. Goodfellow had not had time to start making the hats.

Remember the interesting Japanese couple who lived in our building? They were successful professionals in the city before the war. Their situation was sad. They were forced to be creative to survive. They lived under fear of incarceration, and primarily worked from their apartment. She became a designer and dressmaker and provided my first glimpse into the wholesale market as her model. Appointments with the manager of Polly's on Park Avenue and also with the better dress buyer at the Neiman-Marcus buying office on 5th Avenue made all other jobs pale. Working with the designers and beautiful merchandise, having the chance to be creative and the luxury to travel extensively—it would be difficult to want more.

Emily, you introduced me to the magnificent Riverside Church. I appreciated Dr. Harry Emerson Fosdick's superb sermons. The chimes pierced the air as we walked the two blocks toward Riverside Drive and the church. The organ music by organist Virgil Fox mesmerized us while the sunrays pierced the stained glass windows. We were filled with awe and reverence even before the minister rose to speak. Dr. Harry Fosdick was followed by a Scotsman, Dr. Robert James McCraken. Because it was a non-denominational church, it was able to attract the best ministers of all faiths.

You and I seldom missed attending church, but I vividly recall being "laced down" one cold, rainy Sunday morning when I called you to see if we would be facing the elements to attend church. "Louise," you said, "the South is the only place where people stay home when it rains. Put on your boots, raincoat, and hat. You are in New York City now, act like it."

We lived in the City with the 5th Avenue double-decker bus, the El on 3rd Avenue, the Automat on 5th Avenue, the crowded, stifling subways, the drugstores with signs in the windows: "Cinders Removed— Fifty Cents". How I begrudged spending some of my lunch budget for this uncomfortable procedure.

Every day in New York City was a day filled with new experiences. I lived there in the heyday of the Big Bands. What a rare bonus. Remember dancing under the stars to the Glenn Miller Band? Although the great Glenn Miller had been lost at sea several years earlier, the band had no trouble being booked at the "Glenn Island Casino" up in Rye. Only once did our dates take us to the Meadowbank Club over in Jersey City. The fellows commented that we would have felt safer had they brought a couple of policemen with us. Today the same area is the home of some outstanding restaurants and restored housing. Do you remember when our escorts took us to the Village to observe the "Drag Queens"? What a shocker!

In college I would risk a demerit by staying up to listen to the midnight broadcast of the Big Bands, never once dreaming I would dance to many of them live. Johnny Long's sister was in school with me. We often heard his band at the witching hour.

Many famous bands played at the New York hotels for short or extended engagements, including the Roosevelt, Commodore, Astor, and Biltmore (where we met out-of-towners under the big clock).

Just two blocks toward the City from our apartment was a handsome neoclassical building Butler Hall. Did it belong to Columbia University? After church, we sometimes ate lunch at the Penthouse Restaurant there and we were always on alert to catch a glimpse of its most famous resident—General Dwight D. Eisenhower, president of nearby Columbia University. You saw him the Sunday he spoke at Riverside Church. I had left New York earlier. Thirteen years later, while attending a business meeting at the Beverly Hilton, I was allowed a close up view of the ex-President Eisenhower. Our meeting had recessed for a mid-morning coffee break in the hotel lobby when the security appeared from nowhere and set stanchions in front of the stalled elevator bay. Minutes later, we were greeted by the uniformed general, ex-President of the United States, as he was rushed away by his bodyguards. I was struck by the fact that he was not as tall as his photographs and movies would have you believe, but he was a handsome, well-groomed man.

The only New Year's Eve I ever spent in New York, we had reservations to dance at the Aster and watch the ball drop at midnight. The name of the band escapes me, but it could have been Artie Shaw, Tommy Dorsey, Woody Herman, Benny Goodman, Harry James, or Les Brown. (Could we have been jaded?)

I am reminded that we met Fred and Ralph at the Sloan House YMCA at a Friday night dance when you had been invited to be a hostess and had been allowed to include me. Although recently returning from the war, neither man wanted to talk about it. Fred's parents were involved in the fashion business and he and I shared many interests.

Besides lots of dancing, Fred and I saw all the better movies and shows at Radio City Music Hall. One night I commented that most movies did come south, but one had to come to New York to see a Broadway show. On our next date, Fred announced that he had bought tickets for every good play on Broadway; three sets of tickets a week for the next two weeks. The only ones that I remember were "Oklahoma" and Lillian Hellman's "Little Foxes". Few people are so thoughtful. Then, though, I don't think I fully appreciated it.

Emily, we were in New York at the right time—never a dull moment!

Love,

Lauren

Chapter Four

Fascinated With Retail —
Fascinated With New York

Dear Emily,

I knew I had found my niche when I went to work on a flying squad at Lord & Taylor. Fresh orange juice and coffee were served from a silver service every morning in the sheltered entrance. The ladies were assisted from their cabs or limousines by immaculately groomed doormen. I attended merchandising classes at New York University two nights a week. Classes were taught by buyers from Macy's and Bloomingdales.

From the first day, I was sure that Lord & Taylor was different, but I was not prepared for all that happened. One cold, blustering spring morning we arrived to find the street floor transformed into a fairyland. Fifteen twenty-foot blooming cherry trees were planted in huge wooden barrels and were spaced down the three aisles. A delicate perfume permeated the air. On holidays, an organist played from the balcony. Interior displays supported the fashions of the season. For me, everything associated with the store reflected exquisite taste, from the green awnings with the Lord & Taylor long-stemmed rose to the smallest accessory inside.

My favorite location was the Young New Yorker shop on the sixth floor where Anne Fogarty's billowing petticoats underpinned voluminous skirted dresses. Made from beautiful natural fabrics, these dresses carried more appeal than any dresses I had known. Neither junior nor missy, 7th Avenue had finally targeted a customer who had been overlooked, and brought new life to the drab dress departments. Soon accessories followed to complete the look.

The advertising format was unique for its time and influenced the advertising in stores from east to west. The free-flowing, airy style was in opposition to the tight format used by most stores. The windows were by far the most outstanding in the city. On Thursday nights between 8 p.m. and 9 p.m., many people would be waiting outside for the displays to rise (mannequins were dressed on the lower level and all displays were elevated on cue). Often fashion windows had twelve to fifteen mannequins presenting the same fashion statement. Merchants came to see; designers came to sketch; and everyone found inspiration in the fashion execution. A fascinating Christmas display was the miniature facsimile of the store in the mid 1800s. The eight-floor facade was a large lighted tree.

One April morning, a well-dressed lady stopped by the handkerchief department to purchase an all-over embroidered linen handkerchief for one dollar, asked to have it gift-wrapped, cashed a check for $100 so that she would have lunch money, and requested to have her full-length black mink coat sent to her Park Avenue address. She would be meeting a friend for lunch at Club 21. The temperature had risen which made her long coat a bother. Every detail was met within minutes, accompanied by a smile and a "thank you".

Dorothy Shaver, the forty-something-year-old president of Lord & Taylor, arrived by cab each morning twenty minutes before the store opened. She wore a black dress or black suit and made her way through the handbag department en route to the eighth floor express elevator. She called many of the sales girls by name (everyone at Lord & Taylor was referred to as either "Miss" or "Mr.". I had thought this only a Southern custom). Often Ms. Shaver would stop for a chat and ask about the families. She had started as a comparison shopper and progressed up the ladder, but she did not forget her former friends.

It was at one of her evening self-improvement classes that I was first introduced to opera. A knowledgeable person from the city's music world discussed "Carmen" while we listened to the recording. Not long afterwards, you and I brought our bedroom slippers down to work, bought a standing room ticket for a dollar and saw the real "Carmen" at the old opera house. Was it West 39th Street? What better way to be introduced to opera than a night of "Carmen" with Risë Stevens?

Sunday afternoon outings took Fred and me to Fort Tryon Park, the Cloisters, Bronx Zoo, and the 5th Avenue museums. The organ music at the Frick Museum was the perfect background for contemplating the Old Masters, and the Frick was not as bewildering as the Met. The Vermeer was my favorite. You knew the Little Rock, Arkansas girl, Blanche, who was librarian at the Frick Museum.

Someone in our group commented that Southern girls seemed to be favorite social secretaries, especially if they included Katherine Gibbs in the resume. Your friend, Alma, was social secretary for Mrs. Francis DuPont in Wilmington, Delaware. One weekend the two were in New York and invited you to join them for high tea at the Waldorf on Saturday afternoon. I don't know how I rated an invitation unless it was to prevent you from traveling alone, but we put on the best we had and met Mrs. DuPont and Alma on the Waldorf balcony. I was nervous as a kitten, but managed not to spill anything. Although I do not remember how Mrs. DuPont looked, I recall that she was warm and made one feel comfortable. It was a double feast—one for the eyes and one for the taste buds. After we completed our dainty sandwiches and an assortment of cakes, Mrs. DuPont turned to Alma and asked how much tip she should leave. I had a North Carolina friend from Rockingham who was social secretary for Helen Hayes. One of her assignments was to drive Mrs. Hayes back and forth between her Nyack home and the theater.

Another Southerner seeking to make her mark in New York was Jerri from West Virginia. After getting her M.A. in food service at Columbia University, she worked in her chosen field at Schrafft's Restaurant, a popular lunch and tearoom. Some locations served dinner. Plans were underway for her to marry an older man who was seeking a musical career when I left the city. Not long after they were married, she lost her parents in a tragic automobile accident. Since she was the only heir, she sold the apple orchards in West Virginia and bought two or three grand apartments in the fashionable Hotel des Artistes off Central Park at 1 West 67th Street. The couple occupied one apartment while you and others from Morningside Drive moved into another.

Few working girls were so lucky. I would have loved to be so fortunate. I think I visited you only once on a return trip, but I can still vividly see the entrance into the spacious room with an extremely tall, vaulted ceiling. The architecture was Jacobean. There was an enormous stone fireplace with an exposed chimney that climbed to the twenty-five-foot ceiling. It had leaded glass windows that filled much of the outside wall, and wide, dark oak floors throughout. The tiny bedrooms and bath were situated on the balcony and afforded little privacy. One bedroom and bath fit snugly behind the main room. Daylight flooded the downstairs, which was perfect for the artist studio for which it was designed.

Probably fifteen years later, I had occasion to visit another apartment in the same building. Louise Murray, V.P. of Fashion Sportswear at A.M.C. (Associated Merchandising Cooperation), Thalhimers' New York buying office, shared the large apartment with her artist brother. The living room was smaller than yours, but the sky-lit studio was enormous and was filled with canvases in different stages of completion. He had painted several presidents, including Eisenhower, Kennedy, and Nixon. He always interviewed his subjects in his studio and, if an agreement was made, he painted his clients in their surroundings. Lyndon Johnson was the only President from whom he rejected a commission. Their personalities just did not mesh.

The Hotel des Artiste Restaurant on the ground floor was one of New York's most popular in the 1970s and 1980s when I was fortunate enough to be wined and dined there. The proximity to Lincoln Center should assure its prospering.

Betty, from Fair Bluff, North Carolina, arrived in New York via Langley Field and NACA, enrolled at the Artists Student's League, and soon was designing and illustrating children's books at Scribner's. The younger

Mr. Scribner was killed in a plane crash just weeks before his planned wedding. The charming East Side apartment he had bought and decorated was offered to Betty while the family made some decisions. Remember our visit?

Betty made a ritual of working in a top publishing house for a few years and then taking a sabbatical to Europe to paint for a sun-drenched year. Her first painting year was spent in Greece. She preferred renting from a family where she could learn the language and customs of the natives. She went to work for Harcourt, Brace, & World, followed by a stay in Italy. I believe she had a second tenure with Scribner's. No doubt she was so highly qualified that finding another job was no problem.

Probably the smartest person I have ever known, Betty aimed to read a book every day. Betty was a beautiful young girl, a smart dresser (Bergdorf Goodman customer), and well liked, but she had little time to cultivate friendships. The last time I visited her, she was living on the East Side not far from the Met. There were many canvases, all turned to the wall. She later rented a studio in the same neighborhood. I kept thinking she would have a one-woman show. If she did, I never knew about it. Betty was such a perfectionist that she was unable to appreciate and share her own work. It had to have been outstanding. I wonder if her brother, sponsor, or any members of her family were allowed to share her accomplishments.

New York proved to be more exciting, interesting, stimulating, motivating, and challenging than I could have imagined, a post-graduate course in life. Exposure to the best museums, theater, music, churches, fashion, food, and general good taste made a lasting impact on my life. I am indebted to you for your support in my undertakings and for introducing me to people and places. New York could just as easily have been a lonely, frightening place. Much as I loved living in New York and later doing business on 5th, 6th, and 7th Avenues, I was never sure that I wanted to spend the rest of my life in such a large, cold space. I think I missed most the trees, grass, and big outdoors. You must have shared my feelings when you returned to Chapel Hill to get your degree in Library Science and to work in Richmond, Virginia.

I treasure the many new friends I acquired while living in New York.

Love,

Laura

Chapter Five

Lord & Taylor

Lord & Taylor headquarters and flagship store
on Fifth Avenue in New York City

 Dear Emily,

Here's a little more about our favorite store—
enjoy!

Lord & Taylor can trace its beginning to Lower

Manhattan in 1826. A. T. Stewart opened the same year. It was not until years later that either could be termed a true department store. For longevity, Lord & Taylor is the oldest store that evolved into a department store in this country. Born in the county of Yorkshire, England, Samuel Lord was orphaned early. At age twenty-three, he married his employer's daughter, borrowed $1,000, came to America, and opened a store.

Because of his dedication and industry, Samuel Lord was able to enlarge the store the first year and take a partner, his wife's cousin, George Washington Taylor. So successful were the two that Mr. Taylor decided to take his fortune and retire to Manchester, England in 1852.

With the population movement uptown, the store's destiny was determined. In 1872, Lord & Taylor moved to Broadway at 20th Street into the first iron frame building in New York. A steam elevator was installed to transport the ladies to all five floors. The handsome new building was given much publicity and compared with Worth of Paris.

In 1903, Lord & Taylor made an entrance on 5th Avenue and Broadway. Through several planned moves, the store had gone from Catherine Street to the Bowery, to pioneer an uptown area. Eleven years later, the store moved to its present location—5th Avenue and 39th Street. This location is historic, having been the scene of a battle of the Revolution. General Howe was delayed by Mrs. Murray (of Murray Hill) while Washington and his troops escaped to Harlem Heights.

In 1914, the completed building was state-of-the-art and over the years has claimed many merchandising firsts: first electrical Christmas display, first quick lunch counter, first shops appealing to short women (now petites), teenagers, and college students. The exterior is a handsome structure in Italian Renaissance style executed in limestone and marble and has an air of timelessness.

For thirty years, Edward P. Hatch guided the company. At his death in 1909 part interest was sold to United Dry Goods Company (later to become Associated Dry Goods Company). Management went to his grandson, Howard P. Hatch. The next ten years were difficult as a $6 million building debt was repaid.

In 1926, Lord & Taylor celebrated its centennial with the following editorial:

Making the Practical Picturesque

"Beauty was in the world long ago, but only the rich and powerful could enjoy it.
Today nearly everyone may be rich and powerful as far as beauty is concerned.
The world is coming into its inheritance and this store is one of the Trustees of
Beauty's Estate.

Under Walter Hoving, president from 1935 to 1945, Lord & Taylor became one of the most stylish stores in the world. After graduating from Brown, Hoving drifted before joining R. H. Macy & Company's rigorous training squad. At age thirty, he decided what he wanted to do. He enrolled in night classes at the Metropolitan Museum of Art and studied painting, color, textile design, old silver, and rugs until he felt his background was complete. While serving as a chairman of the board of directors of Lord & Taylor, Mr. Hoving became its president.

"The importance of design in moving merchandise has been something of a fetish with Hoving", wrote

"*Business Week*". His interest in design resulted in his establishment of awards for outstanding work in merchandise design. "We must have original designs and not just copies of higher-priced things ... to build a great trade in clothes designing in this country," said Hoving. "Originality wore no price tags." After leaving Lord & Taylor, he headed Hoving Corporation which was comprised of fine specialty stores. It was his theory that the emphasis should be on the store differences rather than standardization as today's merchants stress. (If he thought there was a lack of creativity then, what would he think of the mass merchandising of today? Who made the decision that every woman wears a medium-width shoe? Have you tried to find a well-tailored woolen pair of pants? Who buys all the acetate and polyester combinations in all classifications?) Bonwit Teller and Tiffany's were two examples of his doctrine. Bonwit no longer exists.

With Dorothy Shaver as president, Lord & Taylor was the most creative store in New York in the 1940s and 1950s. ("Bloomies" was a late bloomer). It was her idea to promote American designers when Paris was the vogue. Claire McCardell, (I bought one of her great black dresses while working at L & T), Bonnie Cashin, and Anne Fogarty owed much of their success to her loyal support. Under her leadership, the windows and the advertisements were in a league of their own. The Young New Yorker shop on 6th was a complete store for the sophisticated gal long in advance of the competition. Years later "Bloomies" retaliated with its East Side Shop.

Ms. Shaver joined Lord & Taylor in 1924 as head of the Comparative Shopping Bureau. Soon she was providing personal shopping on a one-to-one basis, introducing the Personal Shopper. During her first few months with the store, she submitted an unsolicited report to the president, analyzing what was wrong with the company and how to correct it.

Soon she was given more responsibility. Her innovations earned her membership on Lord & Taylor's Board of Directors. Elected President in 1945, she was the first woman to head a major retail establishment in the United States. Her death in 1959 ended her era, but her legacy and innovative concepts earned her a berth with John Wanamaker and Marshall Field as this nation's finest retailers.

Across town, the construction of the 3rd Avenue El in 1879 brought customers to Bloomingdale's door. The store catered to a conservative middle class clientele looking for value at a price. Ironically, the removal of this same El in 1954 and a complete change in the profile of the neighborhood created a fabulous, fashion-forward "Bloomies" of the late 1960s and 1970s. It became the popular place to see creative displays—especially the Home Store rooms—and forward merchandise, as well as the smart place to be seen on Saturdays.

Some merchants countered that "Bloomies" sold the "sizzle and not the steak", but the new "Bloomies", together with the arrival of a barrage of fine specialty stores catering to the wealthy, impacted the 5th Avenue stores including Lord & Taylor.

The 1960s and 1970s were difficult times for the stores. If you wanted shoes, you went to Saks. If you wanted a dress, you automatically went to Lord & Taylor. During the revolt against the midi, Lord & Taylor had more to lose.

In 1975, Joseph E. Brooks was hired from Filene's of Boston to try to recoup some of the prestige and volume lost to the uptown stores. Under his leadership, the store continued to be a fine store with innovative merchandise and promotions. Associated Dry Goods, the parent company of Lord & Taylor since early in the century, had enjoyed tremendous growth under the direction of William P. Arnold. In five years, sales and earnings had more than doubled. The stock had moved from $16 to $70.

Lord & Taylor was the brightest star in the Associated Dry Goods group and the most innovative in New York. Between Brook's arrival and Arnold's death in 1984, the store had expanded from eighteen units, mostly in the Northeast, to forty-two stores countrywide. Sales had more than tripled and earnings had more than quintupled. Associated was one of the darlings of the industry when May Company of St. Louis decided they wanted to acquire them.

The two companies were opposites. Associated encouraged an independent style of operation that supported creativity. May Company believed in strong central control that made for dull, cookie-cutter, and middle-of-the-road stores. With nothing reminiscent of Lord & Taylor but the nameplate, May Company attempted to take the chain national and opened stores as far west as Denver.

After weak results and repeated tinkering with the merchandise, May Company failed to make a statement. Lord & Taylor ceded its former leadership role to Saks, Neiman-Marcus, and Nordstrom—specialty stores. A new CEO tried to salvage the chain by announcing the closing of thirty-two unproductive stores. The new leadership sought a return to the store's roots. Focus was placed upon creating an upscale shopping experience in the remaining fifty-four locations. With all the damage that had been done in the last twenty years, the task was an enormous one.

Three years later, May Company was acquired by Federated Department Stores who soon announced the sale of Lord & Taylor. On June 22, 2005, Federated announced that NORC Equity Partners LLC would purchase Lord & Taylor for $1.2 billion.

It is a sad commentary when the finest store of this century can be taken over by a group such as May Company or Federated with no prior experience in quality merchandise. Only someone who underestimated the savvy of the Lord & Taylor customer could have made this move.

When Lord & Taylor had been written off by its former customers and by fellow retailers, an unexpected revival took place...a most striking turnabout. The 182-year-old store is again a bustling fashion contender. Mr. Baker, from the buyout firm of NORC and Ms. Ellers, a chief executive already in place, are credited for the transformation. They view Lord and Taylor as now positioned well above Macy's, between Nordstrom and Bloomingdale's and under Neiman-Marcus and Saks. More than 200 new upscale lines have been added. Customers are tired of the entire look-the-same conglomeration where most branded merchandise has been replaced by private labels. So far, the acceptance has been good.

If this approach succeeds, more stores will follow suit and shopping could once more be fun and rewarding. Creative New York houses could reclaim some of the China trade. I loathe seeing an Ellen Tracy made in China…not for me!

Love,

Laurie

Part Two:

Back to Charlotte, North Carolina

Women Are Going Places —
And Getting Paid for It, Too!

By Velma Jean Clary
Staff Reporter

Travel and work go hand in glove for some women.

Among them are five in this area who accept the travel to get the work, or accept the work to get the travel.

Mrs. May Belle Jones usually travels between two widely-separated enterprises each week.

Late Wednesdays, she leaves her job as president and treasurer of an export agency on Fifth Avenue in New York, and her apartment on the East River.

She arrives by train in Greensboro early the next morning and drives 12 miles to "Trailing Cedar Farm," Summerfield, R. 1, in time for breakfast. With her husband, Roger M. Jones, who is in public relations with Western Electric Co. here, she also manages the 264-acre farm stocked with herd cattle.

Late on Sunday, she leaves the farm and is back at her executive desk Monday morning.

Familiar Sight

Tall, dark-haired Frances Folger at the piano is a familiar sight in Northwest North Carolina.

She lives with her mother in Mount Airy and travels the state, performing at parties, receptions and other social affairs. Frances and two men who make up the combo have played their way, Friday and Saturday nights "all winter," from North Wilkesboro to Chapel Hill.

The combo played for two parties in Winston-Salem last weekend, and she will be resident pianist at Greystone Inn in Roaring Gap during the summer.

A slender, blondish woman, spends working hours poking around houses and other buildings over the state.

She is Mrs. Dottie (Norman W.) Swanson of 621, Yorkshire Road, an editorial scout for magazines such as Popular Mechanics, Progressive Farmer and the House and Garden building and remodeling guides. As such, she submits a brochure of photographs and facts to the editors for possible pictorial feature stories.

Miles and Miles

With a magazine editor, she once traveled 1,900 miles and looked at 12 houses in three days. And on another trip she inspected six kitchens in a week with a photographer and editor.

At the moment, she is scouting for a North Carolina house with a wooden exterior and plaster or sheet rock interior for a story in a trade magazine.

And she is busy on a story and pictures on the Old Salem Restoration for the Louisville-Courier Journal.

Mrs. Ann (Grady) Kirkman of Kernersville manages the Dick Anderson Travel Service here. She has visited 16 countries in Europe and the Near East to look at hotels and restaurants "and get the feel of the cities and countries. It is so much easier to work out travel arrangements of cities where I've been," she said.

With her in the same office is Miss Madge Henderson of 700 Ontario Street,

who was notified on a Thursday that she was going to Jerusalem on Saturday for a week.

A favorite haunt of Miss Louise Thomas of 738 Pine Valley Road is London's silver vaults, where silver from English estates is bought and sold.

As general merchandise manager, she buys all the imports—ladies ready-to-wear and gifts—for Thalhimers de-

partment store here and some items for stores in Greensboro and Durham.

She spends at least one month each year in such places as Paris, Rome, Milan, Zurich and Brussels—browsing for antiques all over, buying knits in Italy.

Besides the European jaunt, she works in New York one week each month, goes to Atlanta twice a year

and travels continually to Richmond, Va., and other nearby cities.

Some of the women took a circuitous route to their present positions.

Mrs. Jones taught college French, lived 13 years in Europe and Latin America, where she studied languages, and was an interpreter at Macy's in New York. Then she detoured into personnel work, executive scouting and, eventually, settled in merchandising and retailing.

In 1956, she moved up to chairman of the board and vice president of New York's Mark Cross, Inc., a leather specialty firm in which she had served as consultant and director.

Her present executive post in the export firm came in 1961.

Miss Folger has stayed by the piano but to various parts of the country. After college and study in New York, she played in clubs in Florida and in the Boston, Mass., area, especially a famous inn on Cape Cod. She called the inn, "the most beautiful place I've ever seen. I've got sand in my shoes for that part of the country."

Studied Craft

Mrs. Swanson studied journalism but she stayed put with her engineer husband and two children until she answered a notice for editorial scouts in a magazine. After the children were "up a bit," she said.

"The only way to learn this work is on the job," said Mrs. Kirkman, mother of two children. She hadn't even flown to Charlotte before her first flight to Europe, but she got along fine. "I waited in Madrid with a map and Spanish-English dictionary," she said.

A Charlotte native, Miss Thomas went to New York after college and worked at modeling and the retail business. She also studied retailing at New York University. After a stint at Ivey's in Charlotte, she came to the store in Winston-Salem.

Packing can be a problem for the most seasoned traveler. Mrs. Jones leaves city clothes in New York and travels with a briefcase and paperback books. Miss Thomas tries to leave room in her luggage to bring home more than she takes.

Rewards Noted

But all five of the women made more of the rewards than of the difficulties in traveling work.

Mrs. Swanson has been inside enough houses to get to know how people really live.

"I couldn't live without my piano," said Miss Folger. "This way I can live at home and do what I like best."

In a matter of hours, Mrs. Jones can be far from city traffic and sitting on the back porch while birds sing their approval of plowed fields, pastures with streams and luxurious green woods.

The lack of extreme fatigue that once accompanied her work she attributes to the complete change of pace.

Who said a woman's place is in the home?

Miss Louise Thomas is always on the go looking for gifts and ready-to-wear that other women will like enough to buy.

Staff Photos by Frank Jones and Bill Ray

Chapter One

Decisions, Decisions

 Dear Emily,

This was the shock of my life!

After eighteen months in New York City, I returned home due to the unexpected death of my sixty-two-year-old mother. Shocked and saddened by losing my mother, I also missed my friends in the city. Feeling a strong allegiance to my family, a month later a cousin and I took the Peach Queen to New York to gather my sparse belongings and to say goodbye to my friends and another way of life. The urge to be there for my father and younger sister prevailed and proved to be the right decision. The next eight months spent with my father and three siblings proved to be quality, memorable time.

Teaching was an option but my fascination with the fashion world urged me to make appointments with the personnel managers at Belk and Ivey's department stores. Both interviews went well, but Ivey's was more fashion-oriented and a more prestigious label in Charlotte and the surrounding areas. Belk was the only department store in many small towns. Saturday shoppers preferred an Ivey's label when they shopped in the city. Although Charlotte proper only numbered around 130,000 residents in the 1940s and 1950s, there lived one million potential customers within a one-hour drive. Mail orders were tremendously popular.

The only opening in a fashion division at Ivey's was as an assistant in the accessories division, which included handbags, costume jewelry, blouses, scarves, umbrellas, and ribbon. The buyer, Miss Etta Pittman, had good taste, was smart, hardworking, and highly respected at home and in the market. She was a splendid teacher.

The departments were being groomed for the holidays when I reported to work in mid-November. I followed in my mentor's footsteps and absorbed all I could. Because Miss Pittman was sick for several weeks after Christmas, I was forced to learn on my own what I had missed.

Soon I was making the market trips to New York with Miss Pittman. I wrote the orders as we both made the selections, thus making possible more appointments each day. Filling in the quantities soon became easy. By evening, we had only to review the dollars allocated on each order and summarize.

Unlike most department stores, the Ivey's buyers were paid on volume and profit. The store rumor was that Miss Pittman was the highest-paid buyer in the company. Belk paid a salary that paled by comparison and incentives were lacking. On the other hand, we were paid a minimal salary and a great bonus at year-end if our efforts had been directed well. I felt like an entrepreneur.

One May/June Miss Pittman and the daughter of Mr. J. B. Ivey (the store's founder) made a six-week boat trip abroad. I was fortunate to make a market trip alone and had no problems. After that successful experience, I started interviewing for buyer positions in the store: lamps, linens, and gifts for the home. However, my interest was only in a fashion department. No compromising, I was happy as an assistant in accessories.

Emily, I enjoyed my exposure to all of these different departments, but jewelry and handbags were my favorites.

Love,

Laura

Chapter Two

Promoted to Buyer

Dear Emily,

Finally, I got my lucky break.

Without warning, the capable, enthusiastic Junior Buyer at Ivey's announced that she and her husband were building a home in the country (now mid-town Charlotte). She was in her early fifties. Her only child had graduated from college, and she was ready for a more leisurely life. Her husband was a sports writer for one of the daily newspapers, but he didn't object to commuting.

As I look back, I realize that much of my success has been timing—right place at the right time. There couldn't have been a better assignment for me. Anne Fogarty, Betty Carol, Anne Klein for Junior Sophisticates, Mr. Mort and Arkay were the most exciting fashion labels in the post-war era, and none were being properly shown in Charlotte! My exposure to their names at Lord & Taylor and my New York trips gave me confidence. It was almost impossible not to succeed. Management told me, the new young buyer (half the age of my peers), that they would be pleased if I maintained status quo. I sensed they felt they were taking a risk in making someone so young responsible for so much money.

My new assignment included all junior fashions: dresses, coats, suits, and sportswear. There was no resource structure for junior sportswear. Occasionally a missy manufacturer would re-size a bestselling item and offer it to junior departments. These items were so well accepted that soon a junior resources structure developed. (Much of misses sportswear was created in response to the request of women who preferred pants for factory work during the preceding war years.)

CHAMPAGNE satin cocktail dress is modeled by Mrs. R. L. Dalton Jr. A bow centers the hem of the full skirt.

CHANEL-INSPIRED beige flannel dress is worn by Louise Thomas. With it the model's a fox muff and fitted cloche.

PHEASANT FEATHER hat and sable scarf add elegant touch to imported wool suit. Model is Mrs. Mary Wells.

My favorite department was a Young Designer Shop targeted at sophisticated gals of all ages in sizes six to sixteen. The department sold more dresses for $39.95 to $249.95 than did the French Room. The regular Junior Department sold dresses for $12.95 to $34.95. My assistant and I seemed to stay on the telephone reordering. I bought and wore all the styles I loved. Anne Parrish, fashion editor at the *Charlotte Observer*, submitted some photos in a statewide contest selecting North Carolina's best-dressed ladies, and I made the list in 1957. Customers had nothing in their wardrobes comparable in the early and mid-fifties. Women were starved for something beautiful after wartime deprivation. Volume, turn, and profits soared.

There was great support from the well-trained sales people, clericals, and assistants. Nothing could have happened without them. Ivey's attracted quality help, many young widows from Myers Park.

When the Ovens Auditorium was given to the city by the store's V. P., Mr. David Ovens, a dedicated supporter of the arts, our sales of dressy dresses, evening coats, and wraps spiraled upward. Prior to the exciting new building, arts functions were staged in a high school auditorium.

Montaldo's and Ivey's had a monopoly on the important weddings in the area. Ivey's bridal consultant asked me to accompany her to a big wedding at the A E Zion Tabernacle located a few blocks east of downtown. An important social event, the 600 to 800–capacity church was filled. I sat on the aisle at the back. The procession and the ceremony went off without a hitch. Then the collection plates were passed. The admonishment to the bride and groom should have beckoned the recession, but instead Daddy Grace, a traveling evangelist, asked the congregation if it had been a beautiful wedding. There was a hearty "Amen." He asked how many would like to see it repeated, as it was too pretty to end so soon. "Amen" resounded, and the bride, groom, and wedding party assumed its former positions and repeated every detail...including the passing of the plates.

Word was that Daddy Grace again left town in one of his twelve black limousines, counting his silver dollars and greenbacks dumped into a tin washtub. Rent was difficult to collect after one of his lucrative visits.

***

The Young People's Group, led by Eleanor Belk, at Myers Park Presbyterian Church was a great leveling for me. After a breathless week caught up in business and travel, I joined a congenial group of singles with common interests. We met at the church on Sunday evenings for Bible Study, lectures, or other timely programs. Later we had dinner either in or out. Often on Saturday nights, someone in the group invited us to her home in town or to a second house on the York River. Some of us would serve a light dinner before an event at Owen's Auditorium. Others would have the group for dessert afterwards. A retreat was held several times a year—often with a speaker. Pawley's Island in May, Blowing Rock in July, and a cruise in January are some I recall. This was a great way for young executives to meet compatible friends without having to "go steady". Years later, I am told the group remains most active. Neither Winston-Salem nor Richmond offered anything comparable. Dr. Jones left as minister at Myers Park to head the Presbyterian Seminary in Richmond. Ms. Jones, his widow, and I joined Second Presbyterian Church in downtown Richmond the same Sunday years later.

Love,

Laura

Chapter Three

The Merchant Prince

Dear Emily,

Let me tell you more about the man I reported to in Charlotte, George Ivey, Jr., grandson of the founder of the store. Both in our mid-to-late twenties, we were half the age of most management. Since we were so young, management would have been happy if we maintained the status quo, but I was determined to do more. After graduating from Duke, he had trained in the Greenville, South Carolina Ivey store. Neither of us had specific training for our new assignments. He was bright and ambitious and we worked well together.

Well-liked, but not without an eccentric streak, he was thrifty to an extreme. On New York trips, he refused to let the porter carry his bag and would insist on carrying mine while I wrestled with a huge hatbox. Tired of arguing with the porters, he began to take only an attaché case for a week in New York. The small bag carried planning sheets, a change of underwear, and an extra pair of socks. When the French Room buyer was traveling at the same time, the two shared a room at the Pennsylvania Hotel. Tom Smith said that George Jr.

lathered his wash-and-wear shirt each night in the shower and washed his socks and underwear. One morning, Tom accidentally knocked a sock off the windowsill. He apologized and told his roommate that he would gladly give him a pair of black socks. George insisted that Tom call the front desk, get the name and telephone number of the room directly under their room (four floors down) and call and arrange to retrieve the lone sock. All for a $2 sock!

He once asked me to call my major manufacturer and request tickets for a new Broadway play. I recall that the salesman at Jonathan Logan replied that "it was like sending coal to Newcastle", but he complied and sent two tickets for the hard-to-get "My Fair Lady" with Julie Andrews and Rex Harrison. The uncanny, embarrassing acquisition didn't deter our enjoyment of the perfectly delightful performance.

I would be remiss not to mention that George Jr. later learned to appreciate the good life when he became president at Ivey's. His sixty-foot yacht, which was docked at Hilton Head, and his adjacent condo were charged to the company, as was his private jet.

Interestingly, George Jr. also learned to copy the handsome Kittinger dining room chair for his new home. After pricing the beautiful artisan chair, he became an accomplished cabinetmaker. Growing up in the Great Depression left its mark on many—the rich and the poor! Resiliency and resourcefulness are the fruits of hard times.

Emily, don't you agree?

Love,

Laurie

The J. B. Ivey & Co. Carolinas Fashion Tour of Europe group is pictured boarding an Air France plane in New York City prior to the recent 17 day visit of France, Spain, French Riviera, Italy and England. They are, first row, left to right: Dr. James Elliott, Miss Margaret Lindler, Miss Margie Haney, Miss Margaret Cannon, Miss Louise Thomas and Tom Smith, all of Charlotte; second row, Mrs. Anne Walters of Greenwood, S. C., and Mrs. Marion Persons of Charlotte; third row, Mrs. S. Ruffin Horne and Mrs. John R. Tolar of Fayetteville; fourth row, Mrs. Elizabeth Prince of Charlotte. Travel arrangements were made by Charlotte office of World Travel Service, Carolina Motor Club.

—7 ABOARD RETURNED PLANE—
Local People Survive 'Bomb'

An Air France Superconstellation bearing seven Charlotte passengers was forced to return to Sydney Airport in Nova Scotia after a report was received that there was a bomb aboard.

A two-hour search by firemen and airline officials failed to turn up any sign of a bomb and the New York-to-Paris airliner took off yesterday 2½ hours after it touched down at the Nova Scotia airport.

"LOT OF THINKING"

Mrs. Elizabeth Prince, a reporter for The Charlotte News, was a passenger on the plane. She said the air was "tense" when word got around that there might be a bomb aboard. "We did a lot of thinking," Mrs. Prince added.

Rolf Chappell, general manager of Ivey's, told The News that his store had three passengers aboard the plane. They were Miss Louise Thomas, Miss Marge Haney and Tom Smith. The three are on a fashion tour of Europe.

Mr. Chappell said he got a telegram from Tom Smith last night telling of the bomb hoax. The telegram said the flight was grounded, the plane searched, and the flight safely resumed. No bomb was found.

Other passengers aboard the plane from Charlotte were Miss Margie Cannon, Miss Margaret Lindler, Mrs. Marian Persons and Dr. James Elliott.

OTHER SCARES

Another plane of the same line was called back Thursday night

for a precautionary check after a woman telephoned the company's New York reservation desk and said there was a bomb aboard one of its planes.

Two other craft, one in Boston, the other in Montgomery, Ala., were also checked and cleared Thursday.

Airport officials in Sydney said they believed last night's bomb tip came from a similar call to the New York office. Air France spokesmen in New York declined to comment on last night's scare.

The flight, carrying 53 passengers and seven crewmen, left New York yesterday afternoon at 1 o'clock and was due to arrive in Paris today at 5:45 a.m.

Chapter Four

First European Trip

 Dear Emily,

Nothing compares to that first trip to Europe. Was your first trip there exciting as well? In 1958, when I was sure that there could not be a better job, something I had only dreamed of happened. Three Ivey's executives: Tom Smith, French Room buyer, Marge Haney, Advertising Director, and I were joined by seven interested customers for a seventeen-day fashion tour of Europe. To encourage overseas travel, Air France and Ivey's, who wished to expand its fashion image, jointly planned a trip that would include couture shows in Paris, Madrid, Rome, and London.

Store principals gathered at the Charlotte Airport for a royal send-off in early July. The first overseas flight for many of us turned out to be more than we had anticipated. While my roommate and I were dressing in our New York hotel, Margaret commented how fortunate we were not to have been on the Air France 3 p.m. flight the prior day. The "Today Show" commentator announced that for the first time a plane had been called back due to a phoned-in bomb threat. It was our same flight number.

Our 3 p.m. departure from Kennedy Airport was uneventful. Since this was before the day of the jet, we were scheduled to refuel in Halifax, Nova Scotia, before resuming our flight to Paris. The trip from New York to Paris was quoted as taking thirteen hours. Today that would take you from San Francisco to Hong Kong.

After taking on 25,000 gallons of fuel in Halifax, we were thirty minutes out when we detected something was wrong. Attendants raced up and down the aisle before the pilot announced that we were going to dump the fuel and return to Halifax. An anonymous caller from New Orleans had warned of a bomb on board our flight. Most passengers remained calm. One young army wife on the way to join her husband in Germany had never flown before and needed some reassurance. We later were told that the biggest threat had been that a spark from the engine could have ignited the huge stream of oil gushing just outside our window.

At the airport, located on an Army base, our bags were opened and searched one at a time. Near midnight, the search substantiated a second hoax and we enjoyed a delicious French meal on our final leg to Paris. Our thirteen-hour trip turned into a tiring twenty-three-hour adventure. The *Charlotte News*, the evening paper, carried a front, half-page story and photograph of the stranded travelers. The paper's foods editor had joined us at the last minute, and she had called ahead to assure the paper we were safe.

Few experiences can compare with that of a first trip to Europe, and Paris was the perfect place to start. The Avenue des Champs Elysees, L'Arc de Triomphe, and La Place de la Concorde were a great introduction. The handsome buildings were black with soot. We saw evidence of cleaning on a few buildings. Four years later most had undergone a more thorough cleaning. We walked past the Eiffel Tower to the Sacré Coeur. The Montmartre area, which was filled with would-be artists in a perfect setting, overlooked much of the city.

At the Louvre, we gazed on Mona Lisa and Winged Victory and headed to the Left Bank to browse among the bookstalls and banter with the aspiring artists. We visited the Gothic Cathedral of Notre Dame and admired the many bridges over the Seine.

We were shocked at the empty Palace of Versailles and were told that many of the treasures had been sent to England for safekeeping before England was engaged in the war. England, however, had refused to return them. (I am happy to report that much of the original furniture is now back where it belongs.) Fine houses and gardens all over Europe are said to be inspired by Versailles. Once I asked a guide where Versailles got its inspiration, and he readily replied, "The Hermitage".

The French government had arranged for us to see a show of Givenchy in the Hotel George V. His clothes were beautiful and lady-like. It is not surprising he later became Audrey Hepburn's favorite designer. The unexpected death of Dior meant that his young associate, St. Laurent, designed the line we viewed.

Follies de Bergere was considered a must for entertainment for the novice, but everything we did was highly entertaining, from Left Bank gatherings to picture snapping. We experienced our first ever visit to a flea market (long before they were introduced in the States), and we were not disappointed. All of us came home with steals. Years later all was second-hand and reproductions, just as here.

Our next stop was Monaco and the Palace, which

welcomed visitors to all areas except the Royal Family living quarters. Princess Grace was living there then. At Monte Carlo, we visited the Paris Hotel, Monte Carlo Casino, and railroad station where "Red Shoes" had been recently filmed. Most of the casino players were rich, older women. We saw nude women sunning on the beach on the Riviera (a first and only time to see). A ride along the Grande Cornice offered a spectacular view of the azure water below.

***

On the flight from Paris to Madrid, we traveled with General Channault and his young Chinese bride, Anna, who later became one of Washington's most famous hostesses. The small plane meant there was only one class. I found my seat to be the second behind and across the aisle from the General. After lunch, he took out his gold toothpick and completed his ritual.

The Palace Hotel was on a different time schedule. Dinner was at nine. Due to extreme heat, business was conducted from 10 a.m. to 1 p.m., siesta from 1 p.m. to 4 p.m., and work resumed from 4 p.m. to 8 p.m. That meant that the clubs came to life after 11 p.m. Ava Gardner was seen by our group at the Flamenco Club with her bullfighter friend who would later leave her a scar she would never lose.

We spent a day in quaint Toledo and immersed ourselves in El Greco's picturesque surroundings. We saw numerous examples of his extraordinary views that he had captured in his paintings. The village retained the look and feeling of many centuries past.

The Prado reinforced our appreciation for Spanish art. Velazquez's "Little Princess" still remains one of my favorite paintings. The best Spanish painters and highly selective collections made this manageable museum one of my all-time favorites.

After an exhilarating morning at the museum, our French guide suggested we have lunch next door on the Ritz patio. Tired of cokes and not wanting wine at lunch, someone suggested iced tea. After a long delay, the waiter approached our guide for an explanation of iced tea. Later he arrived with a beautiful cut glass wine cooler containing a pitcher of tea surrounded by crushed ice. Iced tea was an extreme luxury in Spain in the late 1950s. Ice was scarce in Europe, and iced tea in Spain was a novelty.

In 1958, a first visit to Spain included a bullfight. The excitement of the colorful, crowded arena was contagious until the gory sight of blood dampened our *"Ole's"*. Never again! The matadors, in their colorful attire, were all as handsome as they were brave.

Balenciaga was showing in Madrid. He later showed only in Paris. A young, talented man, he was influenced by the Basque fishermen. His line was a younger, more colorful, less structured line than those we had viewed in Paris.

***

The Excelsior was an ideal location for our four to five days in Rome. The Via Condotti was just minutes from the hotel's sidewalk cafe. Thanks to our French guide, who accompanied us through this stop, not one of us lost wallets or passports. High on our list was a visit to the Fontana Sisters who had just recently designed Margaret Truman's wedding dress. Marge, the advertising manager, thought this would make a timely story when we returned.

In Rome, we bought silk umbrellas with sterling

handles, silk scarves, small leather goods, and accessories for a small boutique in Ivey's. We loved strolling and looking in the shops along Via Condotti.

Louise in Rome in the late 1960s at the Hotel Hassler overlooking the Spanish Steps.

A "Roman Holiday" consumed the remaining time. The Spanish Steps, the Roman Forum, the Coliseum, the Pantheon, the Trevi Fountain—where we went often to leave our coins—St. Peter's Basilica, and the Vatican consumed most of three days. The Pope was at his summer residence, Castel Gandolfo, outside the city. We went there the day we toured surrounding areas.

One night we saw a magnificent opera outdoors. I don't recall the exact location. Probably fifty singers were mounted on horses, and the total effort was dynamic. Impressed to find all the bus drivers, cabbies, and street workers listening to or singing arias from operas, we were reminded of the contrast to Charlotte and Grady Cole!

Goodbyes were said to our French guide. We would have been lost without him. Unlike today, few, if any, of the hotels, train stations, moneychangers, restaurants, stores, or visitor attractions had English-speaking employees. We were fortunate that our guide was fluent in five languages.

After our flight over the English Channel and the White Cliffs of Dover, our group was excited to be on English-speaking soil until a member encountered a Cockney-speaking porter. The Grosvenor House was well located for first timers. Many soapbox orators were in the park. The Marble Arch was a hub for transportation. Our English guide didn't miss a landmark from the changing of the guard, Westminster Abbey, Big Ben, Tower of London, London Bridge, and St. Paul's. The latter was surrounded by craters as if the war had only just ended; London showed heavy scarring in vast areas. The lack of precision of the German bombers thankfully spared the great St. Paul's but demolished everything nearby. Later, I was to witness the same in Milan where its gigantic train station had served as the transportation hub for the Allied Forces. With the exception of the Excelsior

Hotel, every building for blocks around had been destroyed, but not one hit had damaged the big station. The Italians said that all bombs left over from a raid on that area were dumped at the huge structure as the pilots headed home.

Day trips took us to Hampton Court, Windsor Castle, and Shakespeare country. Back in London, we were enthralled by the Dickens surroundings, but found Harrod's and Selfridge's merchandise selections lacking. For evening entertainment, I recall only an Elizabethan dinner and a ballet. The theater was still recovering.

The fashion show at Hardy Ames, designer for the Queen, was unexciting. Portobello Road flea market and the Silver Vaults compensated for any shortfalls in the prevalent English fashions. Tom selected a beautiful Worcester porcelain dessert service for Mrs. Ivey.

Although we had witnessed much poverty in Spain and Italy, children selling single cigarettes and begging on the streets, we were not prepared for the impoverishment of the proud British. Our English guide commented that it must be nice to be rich and able to travel when most Englishmen were fortunate to survive. His Harris Tweed jacket was pre-war. The collar had been turned over, and then covered with suede. His elbows carried suede patches, which he reminded us were fashion in America but a necessity in England. All of his shirt collars had been turned. He reminded us how fortunate to have had no war on our soil during this century. World War I and II had taken their toll on Europe. Due to an unbalanced diet and lack of professional care, many English were still missing teeth or wore bad replacements.

Seventeen fun-filled days had come to an end, and we were waiting at the departure area at Heathrow when we heard a wild commotion on the floor just under us. Hanging over the guardrail, we saw mobs of teenagers screaming, pushing, yelling, falling, and fainting. Rescuers were carrying out limp girls on stretchers. Sirens were screaming. Four teenage boys in dark suits and little boy haircuts had arrived from Liverpool and London was not prepared for what happened. No one in our group recognized the celebrities. This was 1958, and the Beatles didn't come to America until 1965.

Our trip was billed as a "Fashion Tour of Europe." We had witnessed Yves St. Laurent's debut to couture with a directional line, but not one of us would have predicted that the Beatles, not St. Laurent, were the most influential fashion encounter of our trip. The revolting of teens, against anything that conformed, still resonates in the fashion world. That parents had lost control is reflected in the clothes being worn by the young even today. Seville Row, selling "way-out" fashions in London, influenced junior wear on the continent as well as in America.

Emily, an exciting beginning deserved a great ending.

Love,

Laurie

La Place de la Concorde where traffic moves in twenty-eight directions all facilitated by one traffic director without the assistance of traffic lights.

Chapter Five

Travel Trivia

Dear Emily,

Since few Americans were traveling to Europe in the 1950s, I have included a few oddities I encountered. Although I had stayed in many of New York's uptown hotels, my first encounter with a bidet came in Paris. After some discussion, Margaret decided it was a laundry basin and proceeded to rinse out her hose and undies. The issue was settled, much to our embarrassment, at breakfast in the hotel dining room the next morning.

Relics of the war, street urinals formed from corrugated metal cylinders, were most prevalent in Paris, fewer in London. They were approximately four-foot tall cylinders overlapped with space to enter and back out and offered some privacy. Men seemed oblivious to happenings around them. An occupant might be seen enjoying a loaf of bread or reading the morning paper.

The use of waxed paper in toilets was a mystery, unless it was linked to a wartime shortage. Men and women shared the same inside toilets. The man/woman symbols appeared side by side. A coin was required before a stall could be entered. We felt fortunate if we could produce the proper metal. A charwoman offered you a towel for another coin.

It was evident why Paris was the perfumer of the world. Thirteen years after the war, Paris had few dry cleaners, but the natives were still wearing the same woolen suits. We were told that dry cleaning fluids became unavailable early, and Parisians had adjusted to doing without cleaners. Meanwhile perfumeries flourished. I kept thinking that an American dry cleaner would have prospered.

On this trip, we saw dozens of storks and stork nests. Except for three women who had traveled to Europe earlier, none had seen the bird that "brought us into the world". England was the most heavily populated with storks nesting in and around chimney pots, but they were seen in many other countries too. Today, seldom, if ever, one spots the handsome bird balancing on one foot on a rooftop. Storks migrate each winter to their natural habitat in South Asia. The draining of swampland for cultivation has contributed to fewer numbers of storks and added them to the endangered list.

European ground transportation recovered with difficulty. Buses were sparse. Cabs were few, old and shabby. Private automobiles were a novelty. The underground, mopeds, and bicycles moved most people. Walking has always been a higher priority with Europeans. The shortage of automobiles in America was minor compared to that abroad.

I encountered my first three-sheeted beds in Europe and immediately became addicted. Today, only our finest hotels seem to have adopted this simple luxury.

Emily, seldom a day passed when we were not reminded of the effects of the World Wars on Europe.

Love,

Lauire

Chapter Six

Too Good to Last

Ivey's in 1924 at Fifth and North Tryon Streets, Charlotte, North Carolina.

 ear Emily,

Following the trip, I commented to friends that with a job so exciting, I would be willing to work without pay, never thinking this would soon be challenged. Ivey's junior dresses enjoyed the largest percentage gain in volume, turn, and profit of any peer store in our New York-Cavendish buying office. That gain was even better than I had dared to imagine!

The following February the executives were called to an unscheduled meeting by our General Merchandise Manager, Mr. George Ivey, Jr. No one was prepared for his announcement. The decision had been made to enlarge the size of the store by one third. The company owned the space in the back. We should be able to increase the volume by at least one third. Think of the extra benefits! There was one catch. The buyers would make no bonuses for the next five years. When the new store had been paid for, the bonuses would increase with the additional volume. Ivey's cunning way of paying a meager living draw, capped by a large bonus, didn't fit with the new announcement.

A line quickly formed outside Mr. Ivey's office. Only those with family obligations in Charlotte didn't consider moving. I decided to let the smoke settle before making a decision. Having been approached by headhunters in New York, I knew what was available for me. As much as I loved my present assignment, I could not see giving Mr. Ivey five of my highly productive years. Buyers who did not have family commitments moved to greener pastures. The incentives had been blown.

Mr. Ivey, unreceptive to my decision to leave, threw

a book across the room and made some unkind remarks about the firm I was joining. His mother apologized for his overreaction. We parted as friends and have remained so.

Emily, this was difficult to do but I had to make a living now, I couldn't wait five years.

Love,

Laurie

Chapter Seven

Ivey's; More Than a Store ~ an Institution

 Dear Emily,

Did I ever tell you about the Ivey family? I hated to leave after more than ten years at Ivey's. Mr. J. Benjamin Ivey was born in 1864, the son of a Methodist minister, and was not spared the difficulties generated by the Civil War. Instead of school, he went to work as an apprentice to a carpenter at age sixteen.

In 1900, he opened a small store in Charlotte after several years of retail experience in nearby smaller towns. The second largest city in the state already had a Belk store with the opening slogan, "The Cheapest Store on Earth". The first two years were lean, but his honesty and frugality paid off. In 1904 he was joined by Canadian, David Ovens, whom he credited with the vision and ambition to build a larger store. Rather than compete with Belk, they decided to target a more affluent customer.

Business boomed and in 1914, Ivey's moved into a five-story building with a dining room and soda fountain—a pacesetter. The first manager of the dining room later opened the S & W Restaurants. Mr. Ivey lent him the money with the stipulation he never opened on Sunday. Mr. Ivey had the windows covered on Sundays. Playing cards or cocktail glasses were not allowed to be sold nor was Sunday travel permitted for buyers.

While Belk promoted "pay cash and buy for less" and followed the railroads into small towns, Mr. Ivey hired a credit manager and made the decision to expand in Charlotte, and later into other large towns. The plan was to concentrate on selling higher-priced clothing to more fashion-conscious customers who expected better service.

The store prospered even in the Depression. Ivey's was known for the sophistication of its buyers, superior selections, glamorous displays, and the courtesy of the sales people. Ivey's was the Carolina's best department store in the 1940s, 1950s, and 1960s. "Meet me on the mezzanine at Ivey's" was an often-heard social invitation.

By 1948, the store had reached $12 million in sales and the owners made the decision to go public. Ten years later the store expanded by a third, but profit margins never regained the former status. Heads of stores in much of the country were caught up in expansion fever. They felt pressured to expand in order to hold a share of the market. The debt load was a strain. Interest rates were at an all time high during the Carter presidency. Rich's, in 1976, and Thalhimers, in 1978, had been sold to larger stores. In 1980, Ivey's merged with Marshall Field's of Chicago fame. Charlotte customers saw no difference except the arrival of the famous Marshall Field's mints. Ivey's remained autonomous. Marshall Field's was a cash-rich company. However, the new President, Angelo Areno, soon managed to squander the assets. Profits plummeted and the company was acquired by Batus of London, a huge tobacco and insurance company, which also owned Saks Fifth Avenue.

In 1989, Batus decided to spin off the retail holdings. There has never been a worse time for a store to be offered for sale along with B. Altman, Bonwit Teller, Bloomingdale's, A & S, Burdines, Foley's, Saks, and Marshall Field's. Whereas Ivey's was estimated to bring between $200 and $250 million, it was sold to Dillard's for $110 million—the steal of the century. Ten years later, Dillard's gave the $5 million downtown store to the city, which turned the handsome building into condominiums.

The Carolinas and Florida lost a fine ninety-year-old institution. The same quality of merchandise and superior service are difficult to find today. The population growth and shift, accompanied by the opening of large malls, made downtown stores huge liabilities. Debt loans with exuberant interest rates made retailing a difficult business, but the ego of Angelo Areno and his poor judgment hastened the demise of Ivey's. Neither did George Ivey Jr.'s private jet, condo, and yacht at Hilton Head help the cash flow.

Long after Richmond and Charleston were thriving, sophisticated cities, Charlotte was still an Indian trading post. Since its beginning, retailing has been the prime reason for Charlotte's being. Not until gold was discovered and mined in the area, did it attract wide attention. After 1825, the gold rush drew outsiders with big ideas. A branch of the U. S. Mint opened in 1837. Charlotte has moved from mining and cotton growing to cotton manufacturing to banking. During the twentieth century, Belk and Ivey's served Charlotte well. Ivey's drew discerning customers from most of

North and South Carolina. Belk attracted those looking for bargains and is now the last family-owned, huge department chain to survive in our nation.

Emily, by now I hope you understand why it was so difficult to leave Ivey's after more than ten years.

Love,

Laurie

Part Three:

On to Winston-Salem,
North Carolina

Dear Emily,

This is an introduction to Mr. Thalhimer who hired me and to whom I reported. Charles G. Thalhimer was born to William Blum Thalhimer and Annette Goldsmith Thalhimer in Richmond, Virginia on June 1, 1920. He was the second of two sons.

After attending Richmond public schools through Junior High, he transferred to St. Christopher's Prep School and graduated in 1937.

The first member of his family to attend college, Charles graduated cum laude from Washington and Lee University in February, 1941.

Newport News Ship Building was expanding and he worked on the Battleship Indiana, four Cleveland Class Cruisers, fourteen LST's, escort carriers, and other projects.

Leaving shipbuilding, he volunteered for the United States Maritime Service. After basic training, then nine months at sea serving as midshipman, Charles returned to the U.S. Merchant Marine Academy and graduated in 1946 as an Ensign U.S.N.R. with a Third Mates license.

His experience at the shipbuilding company prepared him for his return to Richmond where he assisted in the completion of the seven-floor addition to the Thalhimer Grace Street location. Charles's in-store training started in the men's hat department and moved through men's furnishings, children's, and juniors.

In 1948, Charles married Rhoda Rubin Rich from Kings Point, New York. Three wonderful children followed, Charles Jr., Ellen, and Harry.

In the mid-fifties, Thalhimers Richmond decided to expand by acquisition, first with Sosnik's in Winston-Salem, followed by L. Herman's in Danville, Virginia and Ellis Stone of Greensboro, North Carolina. Charles was assigned to the new project. With his vision, enthusiasm, and dedication there soon were fourteen stores that proved to be the more productive division. In twenty years, from 1959 until 1979, the company grew from $20 million to $160 million in volume, $60 million in the NC division. The first Winston-Salem expansion was a store in the Thruway strip that eventually produced $300 per square foot. Thalhimers built stores in Charleston, South Carolina and Memphis, Tennessee before being welcomed to Charlotte, North Carolina.

Management believed in hiring the top New York store architects and supported them. Charles was in charge of location, size, and architecture. I was asked to participate in these planning meetings at home or in New York.

Without his frequent visits, vision, encouragement, support and interest in the employees, and his caring spirit and his interaction with the local patrons, the young North Carolina stores would not have been as successful.

He was elected to the Board of Directors and became the Vice President. During his forty-year tenure, he was General Merchandise Manager, President, and Vice Chairman.

Following in the footsteps of his father, Charles has been supportive of numerous civic projects, and a founding member and long supporter of the Boys Club of Richmond. He was involved in the development and support of the 105-acre garden known as Maymont, he was President of the Jewish Federation, and was also chairman of a successful drive for Muscular Dystrophy.

When the chairman of the Richmond United Fund was assigned to another city, Charles accepted the challenge and exceeded the goal. On the board, he has long been a supporter of The Collegiate Schools. He serves on the Board of the Virginia Museum of Fine Arts and on the Board of the Museum Foundation.

In 1986, he was asked to head the first Capital Fund Drive for Virginia Commonwealth University. A young University, there were few alumni, but Charles beat the $52 million goal by $10 million with $62 million total! Since then he has continued to support the business school, athletic programs, medical division, and serves on the VCU Foundation Board.

When Thalhimers closed, he gave $1 million to a fund to aid the 1,000 employees, many who had never had another job.

Although Charles Thalhimer Sr. retired from retailing in the mid-eighties, he and his second wife, the former Sibyl H. Grubstein of New York City, continue to lead active lives between Marco Island, Florida, Richmond, Virginia, and New York City.

Emily, my job was an interesting, exciting challenge thanks to his support.

Love,

Laura

Chapter One

The Decision Was Not Easy

 Dear Emily,

My decision to take a job with Thalhimers in Winston-Salem was influenced by my desire to stay in North Carolina and after much success at Ivey's, I was ready for another challenge, one that would compensate my efforts. The New York headhunters had kept me informed of interesting openings in the East.

Thalhimers, a large department store with headquarters in Richmond, Virginia had decided to expand by acquisition. Due to the prosperous textile mills and the expanding tobacco plants, North Carolina seemed a good choice. Sosnik's, a fine specialty store in Winston-Salem and Ellis Stone, a department store in nearby Greensboro, were acquired in the mid to late 1950s. The Ellis Stone buying staff was retained but when the prior owner and his wife departed, there were no experienced buyers in the Winston-Salem store. The Richmond store, known as a strong budget operation, was not prepared to cater to the former Sosnik's customers; the merchandise they transferred from the Richmond stocks had been a disaster. The Winston-Salem manager, Sherwood Michael, a former

Richmond sportswear buyer, convinced management to let him set up a local buying staff.

The mid-February Saturday I drove from Charlotte to Winston-Salem for an interview proved to be a shocker. The four-story building covering the front portion of a block was jammed with eager customers. The offerings were disappointing. Fall and winter stock being shown consisted of leftovers from Richmond clearance.

The younger of the two Thalhimer brothers, Mr. Charles, flew down for the interview held in the coffee shop at the Robert E. Lee Hotel. His enthusiasm for the business, his vision, his warm friendly personality, plus Mr. Michael's evident support gave me reason to consider the uncharted future. What if I gave it a year and it didn't pan out? I could always move on. Should I gamble Charlotte, my friends, and the known for a much smaller town and a store lacking history as a department store? A carriage house in Old Salem was appealing. It was not an easy decision.

To one accustomed to running a sophisticated operation with all the support staff in place, this was bedlam. Two years later, we were seeing favorable results and I could at last justify my next move— buying a house. With the help of A.M.C. (Associated Merchandising Corporation), Thalhimers New York buying office, we established departmental resource structures. My experience with Ivey's was most valuable here. How fortunate to have access to A.M.C., the world's largest buying office, whose member stores included Bloomingdale, A & S, J. L. Hudson Company, Dayton's, Rich's, J. W. Robinson, Woodruff & Lothrop, Harrod's of London, David Jones of Sydney, Australia. The best-seller reports from these fine stores were a great support tool. Seasonal meetings with our peers from A.M.C. sister stores were a valuable education.

There was neither security nor a tempting salary to attract experienced buyers. I decided to train various department heads for buying. Delighted to be given the opportunity to expand and learn, most trainees did very well. They became dedicated, motivated and astute buyers who learned to make good decisions.

**

Often I have been asked if I felt discriminated against as a woman in management. My prime example came after two years in Winston-Salem, when I decided to buy a house and went shopping for a loan.

My first stop was a savings and loan where I had an account. I was directed to a loan officer seated midway in the bank lobby. This was 1961, and I was shocked to approach a seated man in shirtsleeves. Then, businessmen wore jackets. He didn't rise, introduce himself or shake my hand. There was only a plaque with his name on it.

I sat down, introduced myself, told him I had worked with Thalhimers for two years and was ready to buy a house. He didn't ask my age, position, salary, obligations or savings. Instead, he asked if I were married, had I been married, and did I have children. Three "no's" summoned a quick reply, "We don't think that women are a good risk." I thanked him and got up to leave. On my way out, I stopped and had a check prepared for the entire balance of my account. The total of that check was more than I wished to borrow.

After calling on two other bankers, who quoted me interest rates, I decided to get my loan from a mortgage banker who offered me a rate below the other two.

Emily, my first house—I am both scared and excited.

Love,

Laura

```
        1962 OVERSEAS TRIP FOR MISS L. THOMAS, SPORTSWEAR BUYER, THALHIMERS, WINSTON-SALEM

   Sat.,      Mar. 31    Lv. New York PA 2, 8:00 p.m.
   Sun.,      Apr. 1     Arr. London 7:35 a.m.
                                                              Connaught

   Mon.,       "   2     In London
   Tues.,      "   3       "
   Wed.,       "   4       "
   Thurs.,     "   5       "  - Lv. BE 358, 7:00 p.m.  fd.
                                Arr. Paris  9:00 p.m.
                                                              Maurice

   Fri.,       "   6     In Paris
   Sat.,       "   7       "
   Sun.,       "   8       "
   Mon.,       "   9       "
   Tues.,      "  10       "  - SK 566, 3:35 p.m.
                                Arr. Copenhagen 5:40 p.m.
                                                              Palace

   Wed.,       "  11     In Copenhagen
   Thurs.      "  12       "    - Lv. SK 637, 5:40 p.m.
                                  Arr. Frankfurt 7:15 p.m.
                                  Lv. OS 402, 8:45 p.m.
                                  Arr. Vienna 10:25 p.m.
                                                              Imperial

   Fri.,       "  13     In Veinna
   Sat.,       "  14       "
   Sun.,       "  15       "
   Mon.,       "  16       "  - Lv. SR 243, 6:30 p.m.
                                Arr. Zurich 8:30 p.m.
                                                              Baur au lac

   Tues.,      "  17     In Zurich
   Wed.,       "  18       "    - Lv. AZ 205, 4:30 p.m.
                                  Arr. Milan 5:15 p.m.
                                                              Excelsior Gallia

   Thurs.,     "  19     In Milan
   Fri.,       "  20       "    - Lv. p.m. train to Florence
                                                              Excelsior

   Sat.,       "  21     In Florence
   Sun.,       "  22       "
   Mon.,       "  23       "(Holiday)
   Tues.,      "  24       "
   Wed.,       "  25       "
   Thurs.,     "  26       "
   Fri.,       "  27       "  - Lv. p.m. train to Rome
                                                              Excelsior

   Sat.,       "  28     Lv. Rome PA 115, 10:45 a.m.
                         Arr. New York 3:30 p.m.

   2/19/62
   mb
```

Chapter Two

New Travel Experiences

Dear Emily,

I didn't expect to start traveling so soon as I had been here only two years, but what's not to love!

After a year in the store, I was sent to Los Angeles to attend a merchandise managers meeting at the Beverly Hilton. This was the first of many management meetings where I was the only female merchant. A.M.C. always sent several women from the New York office, which made me feel more comfortable. The sportswear bought on the Los Angeles trip was successful. For many years, we attended swimwear and sportswear openings in Los Angeles.

The following year, after testing the water by buying and selling all the samples left over from an A.M.C. import fair held in New York, management decided we were ready for the European market. Customer response was reassuring. Few stores were sending buyers abroad. Store principals and top management occasionally took a European jaunt. Mr. William Thalhimer, Sr. and his wife were seasoned travelers and sent home purchases from many countries.

My travels to Europe four years earlier hadn't given me confidence that I was prepared to travel alone to so many uncharted places. Luckily, A.M.C. had a good travel agency and maintained small buying offices in every city I was to visit.

After studying my itinerary, I asked the travel agent if I could switch my London hotel to the Grosvernor House. I had stayed there before and remembered a few helpful landmarks. Since I was to make consecutive trips each spring through 1976, I shall give you my first impressions and move forward to include highlights from my many working trips.

I was welcomed at my hotel by fresh flowers from Mr. Cannon, manager of our London office. Our London office was located on Brook Street, just opposite the Claridge Hotel. At first, gifts and antiques were the favored areas with the American buyer. Later we bought hand-knit sweaters, kilts, and casual jackets. The out-of-town trips to the antiques dealers in Bath, Dunstable, and St. Albans were preferable to a day in Birmingham, a smoky, dingy, industrial city where we bought brass. Remnants of the Roman Wall in St. Albans, the magnificent Crescent at Bath and George IV's Palladium at Brighton Beach are some of my most treasured memories of rural England.

We bought great kilts from Mrs. Moss, who had researched and reproduced every clan on record. Her vast stockroom was an education in Scottish history. Hand-knit fisherman sweaters made in Ireland, were brought into London and shown in our office. Each sweater carried a note with the name of the knitter and the hours she spent on the garment. Most patterns were named. Contractors distributed the yarn and patterns most often to rural women who regularly spent forty to fifty hours on a handsome last-a-lifetime sweater with the natural oils that repelled water. In the 1960s these finely crafted items sold back home for from $80 to

$100; now the price is two to three times that. The contractor was responsible for selling and distributing the money and more yarn. He provided an opportunity for housewives to have a small income.

We later stayed at the nearby Dorchester where we loved to have high tea at 5 p.m. and "people watch." We talked with Johnny Cash once on the elevator there. Breakfast was special in my room in front of a fire. The portable breakfast table would be set with at least a dozen matching pieces of beautiful English bone china as well as fresh flowers.

Later we moved to the Connaught, a smaller hotel built around a circular stair, which allowed every room to have an outside view. I recall only one other hotel similarly built. That was a downtown Lisbon hotel commissioned by one of the kings as his city residence. His trains pulled into the station and he was escorted inside with no public exposure. Both were five-star hotels.

We found the English to be delightful but not the best business people. They repeated the same styles, colors, and fabrics year after year. We explained that we served the same people, and they expected something different. It seemed the directors made all the decisions since they furnished the money. It was evident that the war had left its mark by the color choices in selected fabrics. France, Germany and England continued to show only dark, drab, somber colors, while Denmark and Italy exploded with the pastels and bright colors the South had long embraced. China, silver, brass, men's gifts, and antiques remained the winners from England.

Management encouraged us to absorb as much of the local culture as possible. Banker's holidays, every quarter, offered us long weekends to explore much of the countryside. Oxford, Stratford-on-Avon, Coventry Church, Brighton Beach, and Richmond were a few places I recall. Portobello Road and Chelsea flea markets could easily consume a Saturday.

At the top of our list for evenings was the London Theater. Irvin, who traveled from Richmond, was a Little Theater actor and was in charge of ticket purchases. The first night we arrived in London, he purchased tickets for each of the following nights. On Saturday, he attended three shows. I made other daytime plans. For fifteen years, we saw the best of London shows. Often we would see the American version several years later in New York City. How vividly I recall Sir Lawrence Olivier in O'Neill's "Long Day's Journey into Night", Deborah Kerr in "Day at the Fair" (great), the Redgrave sisters (several times), and Ingrid Bergman in "The Constant Wife", just to name a few of the many actors and productions we were privileged to enjoy. Each year in the 1960s, there seemed to be another satire involving the Royal family. The Duke and Duchess of Windsor were prime targets for many humorous evenings in the London Theater.

We never failed to shop Harrod's and Selfridge on each trip. For years, Harrod's coded their merchandise, which tended to annoy me because one had to ask the price. After the new ownership, Harrod's never regained its former status. Today, neither of the former greats would pass as a fine department store though better than those that survived the American tragedy.

After a busy week in London, the following weekend was spent in Paris shopping and window-shopping. The French have a way with windows. The boutiques used no mannequins; their art of draping gave third dimensions to the simplest objects. We were aware of any fashion trends we could have translated at more popular prices.

There could have been no better selection for a hotel than the Maurice. Located on the Rue de Rivoli, the side entrance (since changed to main entrance) faces the Ritz. Across the street, the Tuilleries Garden housed a museum of impressionist paintings with a fabulous collection of Van Gogh's. Whenever I could spare a few minutes, I would stop in and feel rejuvenated after a short visit there. Nearby was the Place de la Concorde where the Lor Gendarme Ric hand-directed traffic in twenty-eight directions. If there were any accidents there, I never saw them.

The A.M.C. office was in the next block from the Maurice and proved most helpful. They arranged for me to attend at least one couture show each visit (without the required purchase). We were not ready for the collections, but the influence was valuable. My first year, I attended the Nina Ricci show for an elegant, dignified clientele. Over the years, I missed only one show on my preferred list—Madame Chanel, who always opened later than the others. She rebelled against the heavily structured fashions being shown by her contemporaries. Only after America embraced her unstructured designs was she welcomed into the realm of high fashion. I did buy some hand-knit copies of Chanel suits that sold well in our store for $500 to $600. A Chanel suit is never dated. Her influence on sportswear is still felt.

Not until the days of prêt-a-porter did we see our French purchases become meaningful. When St. Laurent opened his first Rive Gauche prêt-a-porter in 1966, it was his way of making an economic statement that there were many women interested in French fashion at below couture prices. A Prêt show was staged in large tents each spring in Paris and attracted better lines from other countries as well. Most A.M.C. stores were represented at these annual shows.

Maurice Hotel Paris, France 1962

My office representative in Paris did not have many appointments for me, but we did not squander the days. She planned her evening meal after stopping by to pinch the hanging plucked chickens and checking all the vegetables at the green grocers. Then the French did not believe in refrigerators. Every portion was bought the day it was to be served. Before I treated her to a good lunch, my guide and interpreter knew what she would serve her husband for dinner. In every city, the office representative knew all of the best restaurants for lunch and made reservations if needed. Otherwise, I would never have known about the best local food. When I traveled alone, I ate dinner in our superb hotel dining room. Otherwise, we had a restaurant list. We saw a table of Americans at one of the fine Paris restaurants. One man was wearing a Western hat and cowboy boots! Is it any wonder that some Parisian restaurants restrict the number of American reservations they accept?

On Saturdays in Paris, I loved visiting the shops and galleries on the Left Bank. On my way back to my hotel, I visited the antique shops on Rue de Rivoli. One incident I shall never forget. As I entered a familiar shop, I was advised that I would love some pieces of Gallé glass for my collection—all Americans loved Gallé. When I replied that I did not collect Gallé, she wanted to know what I did collect. I told her I preferred American, but I also bought eighteenth century English furniture, and Chinese and Oriental accessories. She told me I was wasting my time and money investing in any American furniture and fine arts. "French, Italian and English furniture and accessories have a market all over the world—American is respected only in America." The same year, Barbara Babcock who was the granddaughter of R.J. Reynolds, her father, and Thomas Hoving were making major purchases of paintings from the Hudson River School and other New England artists. American art was just on the cutting edge and their purchases for the Reynolda House Museum have escalated to extreme heights in value. At about the same time, a Philadelphia wing chair brought the highest price for a piece of antique furniture to date. At that time, there was no mass media as there is today. The French were not aware we were on the crest of the wave of acceptance of American art, furniture, and fashion.

Often I am asked who my favorite fashion designer was. I had two favorite designers–Yves St. Laurent and Coco Chanel. After the unexpected death of Dior in

1957, I saw the first line that St. Laurent did for the House of Dior in 1958. With his youth (first line debut at twenty-two), he brought a reckless creativity in contrast with the older, entrenched designers. The midi, the maxi, and the increased dependency on trousers and pantsuits are where his influences are still seen. When he opened his magnificent salon in the mid 1960s, the young man slid down the three-story banister and took his bow amid wild applause. He made his creations available to a wider audience when in the early 1970s, he opened more than twenty YSL ready-to-wear boutiques worldwide. His Italian woolen challis used in this line were unchallenged and contributed to the financial success of the bright, astute designer.

Coco Chanel, who elected to go it alone, left more icons than did any other designer. Her unstructured comfortable clothes, with the use of many knits, influenced the way women will dress forever. The Chanel suit in all of its versions is timeless. The extravagant use of pearls, two-tone pumps, the quilted leather shoulder bag, the wrist-length glove, and her perfumes – especially number five, are with us still.

Midway in my trip, I would receive a letter from Mr. Michael bringing me up to date on all the good news in the store. He always included a "thank you" for all that was going well. He and Mr. Charles Thalhimer were great supporters of mine. I could always count on them making my job enjoyable. Without them, I doubt I would have remained with Thalhimers as long as I did.

***

The flight to Copenhagen took me to yet another culture, one more akin to home. Hand-knit sweaters from Jules Christiansen, fur-trimmed weather coats, ski jackets, pants, sweaters, machine-knit dresses, and suits were well-styled, reflected fresh colors, superior quality, and were welcomed by our customers. The Micki Moto influence was widespread. Whether in a home or in the showroom, in Copenhagen, one couldn't remove her coat until someone appeared with a pot of strong coffee and a tray of melt-in-your mouth pastries.

The Royal Ballet in Copenhagen reminds me of the opera in Vienna. Happy families seemed to be having a once-in-a-lifetime experience at the intermission. "Swan Lake" was performed to a full, enthusiastic house. The dancers were superb, and the audience was the most appreciative I can recall. People were hungry for the experience. There were no performances during the war and for many years after, so I was thrilled to be part of the celebration. I eagerly anticipated attending The Royal Ballet each spring for fourteen consecutive years.

On my first trip to Copenhagen, I was booked at the Palace, which gave me a down mattress and a down comforter for sleeping. With no way to regulate the heat, I opened the windows, unbuttoned and removed the linen duvet cover, and crawled into it as a bottom and top sheet. I was awakened early by clicking noises outside my window. Looking, I saw the Hans Christian Andersen statue in the middle of a traffic circle of bicycles. There was not a car in sight. The bicycles were obeying a traffic light. Scars of World War II were different in each country, but no place in Europe had been completely spared.

In Copenhagen, I experienced my first walking street with the interesting shops and the large home furnishings department store and my first hotel sauna. On a Copenhagen trip several years later, I witnessed the headless Little Mermaid, a beloved character created by Hans Christian Andersen. The statue had graced the harbor in front of the yacht club for years. It was readily replaced.

I spent one day in the Munich office on my first trip. They were not ready for exporting but I did make two more trips before leaving the German market to the toy and Christmas decoration buyers.

At the Vienna airport, I was met by a cabbie who offered to take me anywhere I wished to go for one Kennedy dollar! Imperial Hotel was my destination. He was ecstatic. "Your President Kennedy stayed there when he visited us recently," he effused.

The next morning, after managing to conquer the open revolving elevator, I arrived on floor number one to find Ms. Smithdeal, the accessory buyer from A & S in Brooklyn. After making her selections, she kindly assisted me in choosing of crystal and jet jewelry for our store. Vienna had limited resources for export.

Of all the cities I visited on the month-long trip, Vienna seemed to have suffered most from the war. There were no young men on the streets, only middle-aged men and most of them were maimed, missing arms and legs. Many had distorted faces. Open craters in the earth were everywhere one looked.

The city tour the following morning showed the extent of ruin. St. Stevens and the area surrounding it were devastated. All four steeples of the world-famous cathedral were either missing or badly damaged. In 1991, the repair of the fourth steeple was still in progress, thirty years from the first time I'd seen it. The shops in the area were sparsely merchandised. However, the famous chocolate and sweet shops existed and were well patronized.

Saturday night, Ms. Smithdeal and I, escorted by one of the jewelry agents, attended a performance of "Die Fledermaus" at the Vienna State Opera House. The Viennese love for the opera was in no way diminished by the outdated and worn clothes. At intermission, we observed entire families enjoying an opera-going experience. Years later, I learned that the Austrian government distributed tickets for each schoolchild to take his/her entire family to an opera each year. Is it any wonder that they grow up appreciating the music that was once provided by and for only the royal families and guests? After "Die Fledermaus", we followed the crowd to the lovely Sacher Hotel, famous for its desserts and hot chocolates.

In Zurich, talented ice skaters floated in the reflected glow of the lights from the opulent Baur au Lac hotel.

Hand-knit sweaters, ski pants and accessories, machine-knit sweaters, and two-piece dresses were available here. Although Switzerland managed to remain neutral during the war, it was not spared its effects. Factories survived but scarcely. The beautiful topography allowed no land for farming and made cities highly dependent on imports for food. Rationing and regrouping of essentials took its toll.

On one trip to Zurich, my associates and I stopped by the front desk for our room keys and were told our belongings had been moved to rooms located on another floor. The Ethiopian leader, Haile Selassi, had arrived for an eye operation and brought his harem along. The five-star hotel had not anticipated sixty extra women.

Dinner in the beautiful dining room consisted of more than five courses and was outstanding. The dancing to a band on the veranda followed by after-dinner coffee surpassed any restaurant in town.

Baur au Lac hotel, Zurich, Switzerland

The picturesque train trip from Zurich to Milan was breathtaking—several feet of snow, lots of tunnels, villagers maneuvering on cross-country skis, housewives airing their bed linens on their balconies, the sun beaming off the drifts. It was a complete fairyland.

How fortunate for me that Ms. Smithdeal's itinerary conformed to mine for three stops. In Milano, she bought leather goods while I shopped knits. In the evening, we attended an opening night gala at La Scala. I can't recall the opera because I was too busy watching the elegant women arrive, laden with jewels, wearing full-length minks, and carrying ermine shawls for the seats. What a contrast between Vienna and Milano! I was reminded of an expression at our house during the war days. "Remember the starving Italians. Clean your plates!" We were told that these ladies were the mistresses we were seeing. The wives were home with the children.

The promenade at intermission was worth the price of the ticket. After intermission, the booing started, and before the curtain fell, at least forty percent of the audience had left. I must hasten to add this was an exception to the rule—but an experience to remember. After the final curtain and weak applause, we encountered many of those who left early at a restaurant in the Galleria across the street. Since the performance had started at seven, everyone went for a late supper. Here, I was introduced to rice a lá Milano—sautéed saffron rice, shrimp, mushrooms, and red peppers. The preparation process is too time consuming to be served anywhere but in gourmet restaurants. Don't expect to find it, and that's really too bad.

Emily, the noon train to Florence gave me time to organize my bookwork and try to visualize my next stop. The Excelsior Hotel, located on the Arno two or three blocks below the Ponte Vecchio was the ideal location; everything one could desire was within walking distance. Huge terra-cotta pots filled with salmon-colored azaleas marked the hotel entrance and continued up the street to a full-blown garden of them in the courtyard, Uffizi Galleria. Florence, Italy and Charleston, South Carolina have similar temperatures; I immediately felt a horticultural kinship.

With the aid of a map, I located Palazzo Vecchio (with its poor copy of "David") the straw market, the fine shops of Gucci, Ferragamo, and Donatello's famous restaurant.

Palazzo Vecchio, Florence Italy

Sunday morning breakfast was served on my balcony overlooking the Arno. Church bells were tolling from every direction. Across the river, I watched the monks leave the monastery for prayers and church. What a magical introduction to what became my favorite city in all of Europe.

After crossing the Ponte Vecchio, lined with small shops, our A.M.C. office was located on the right side in the first block. The Pitti Palace was in the second block on the left side. Until the War, the building that housed our office had been a fine private palazzo with fresco ceilings and handsome woodwork. There was a skeleton of a fine garden in the back.

Our well-run office was headed by Renato Masca, a war hero. Soon all the A.M.C. European officers reported to the Florence office. London and Florence accounted for the largest shipments to the States. All Italian factories had been converted to war production. Our purchases for several years consisted primarily of hand-knit sweaters shown in the homes of the knitters or contractors. It was not unusual to have three generations of Italians gathered around the dining room table, all talking at the same time. Italians have a flair for fashion, and their color sense is unparalleled. The smallest suggestion concerning style or color was pounced upon. They were so eager to please that they would have new samples ready in a day or two. Pictures, sketches, color, or fabric samples were welcome. Mohair was the favored yarn at first, and their original styles were snapped up by our eager customers back home. "Hand-knit" was a big attraction.

Florence proved to be our most lucrative market. In addition to hand-knit sweaters and coats, we soon were able to buy fine gauge merino sweaters and machine-knit dresses. For several years, fashion shows were held each February at the Pitti Palace. Later the shows moved to Milan where the high fashion market gravitated and remained. Handbags, belts, gloves, scarves, gifts, children's accessories, men's sweaters, and men's leather goods attracted many Thalhimer buyers. After the first two or three years, I had a traveling companion or several other merchants from Richmond.

The city on the Arno proved profitable for American stores and buyers alike. For years, eighteen-carat gold jewelry could be bought for $35 an ounce, plus a small fee for labor. Much of it was made by hand. We found leather goods manufacturers who contracted Gucci items we could buy for a song (sans the Gucci stamp). Many buyers came home with Gucci luggage. After the horrific flood in 1966, Gucci moved to fashionable Via Tornabuoni, and the area took on a new life. Florence then was a shopper's paradise.

On the spring 1967 trip, we stayed at the Grand Hotel across the courtyard from the Excelsior, because the first floor of the latter had been flooded and was being renovated. I recall having breakfast at the Grand with Joe King, the Winston-Salem portrait artist who spent part of the year in Florence. Many manuscripts and some art were damaged by the high waters. Luckily, the damage proved not as bad as first anticipated. Years later, many of the restaurants near the Arno had preserved the watermarks to remind patrons of the floodwaters.

In just a few years, I saw Italy take on new dimensions. Fiats replaced the many bicycles and scooters. Probably my second or third visit to our Florence office, I found everyone in the courtyard celebrating the first auto belonging to anyone other than the manager. My young sportswear buyer, who lived with her family and had bicycled eight to ten miles each day round trip, had saved her money and purchased a tiny Fiat with space for two. The celebration was fit for a holiday.

Now, the man on the street was better dressed. Life in quaint Florence was even more joyous. The boutiques prospered from additional visitors. Rome was no longer the highly preferred destination. Many of the knitwear manufacturers built handsome villas in the country and drove imported sports cars. Florence had sustained small damage compared to Milan. Strict building codes have preserved the treasured atmosphere of antiquity. Even today, buildings are remodeled or new buildings replacing existing ones are so well camouflaged that they cannot be distinguished from their seventeenth century neighbors. Interiors have been renovated and updated, but the exteriors remain honest. The sportswear buyer with the new Fiat one day complained that her family was the sixth generation to live in the same home; she longed for modern amenities.

It would be unfair to omit the fine food in Florence. Back of the Excelsior in a hole-in-the-wall was a small restaurant, Sabatini, with family-sized tables and a sawdust floor, which served the very best steak and potatoes. We had to get there early to get a seat. There were fancy restaurants, such as Camilla's and Harry's Bar, and some nights we dined in Fiesole overlooking the city. Donatello's was a must each trip. For lunch, a restaurant under the bridge was also a favorite.

In the mid 1970s, the American merchants in Florence encountered strong competition from the German and Japanese importers. The German economy had recovered to the extent that there was a large pent-up demand for some pretty fashions. Germany was producing precision machinery and Christmas decorations, but not known for fashion. The Germans traveled in small groups but left big orders. The Japanese traveled a dozen or more strong and left tremendous orders. Although there were twenty-eight A.M.C. stores, each traveled and shopped separately and wrote separate orders. It became difficult for individual stores to compete for prices and delivery against such competitors, although we had supported the Italian manufacturers through their recovery.

New York manufacturers, aware of competition and rising prices, were taking Italian and French samples to Hong Kong to be copied. Asians, while not known for their creativity, are the world's best duplicators. After a few seasons of buying Hong Kong imports in New York, we decided to build on our own past experience and eliminate the New York importers.

Emily, I will tell you more about that later.

Thalhimers' support of the European market set it apart from the competition. Ivey's childrens divisional made several European trips. Rich's never developed a strong overseas presence. The manager of our Copenhagen office said that we were the only A.M.C. store to have made fifteen consecutive visits to Copenhagen. He concluded that the heavy turnover in management required concentrating on home markets allowing no time to develop European resources.

Europe gave us good quality, innovative and exciting merchandise not found elsewhere. The Orient provides cheaper merchandise and more of it, poor fabrics, and poorly sized and constructed garments. Emily, I think that when the public gets tired of "throw away" merchandise, we will see more "made in America."

Love,

Laura

Athens, 1965

Chapter Three

Goodbye to Sir Winston Churchill

Dear Emily,

I wish you could have been with me on Thursday, January 28, 1965. I did a full day's work at the office in Winston-Salem, North Carolina and then caught an evening flight to Newark and a helicopter to Kennedy airport for an 8 a.m. flight to London. We were scheduled to begin our spring buying trip in Rome, but at the last minute, we were able to switch our destination from Rome to London to attend the funeral of Winston Churchill. Travel was so much easier then. The flights going over were less than half filled in January and February.

At Kennedy airport, I was met by John Christian of Thalhimers Richmond division. A hurried "good morning" was followed by a mutual resolve to attend the funeral of our beloved Winnie who had died earlier in the week. We knew we couldn't attend the services, but we hoped to be as close as possible to show our respect. John and his wife, Polly, were traveling companions for several later European business trips.

Later John Christian became the President of B. Altman's.

The wind was bitter when we arrived at the Ritz Hotel in London. This was my first and only time to stop here. The Doncaster and the Cannaught were much more conveniently located and more comfortable.

We wasted no time in checking in and having dinner in the hotel dining room. After layering shirts, sweaters, jackets, coats, scarves, and gloves we gave the doorman our destination, Westminster Hall, where the body of Sir Winston Churchill lay in state.

The queue, four persons wide, wrapped around Westminster Abbey. Emily, you know how terrible January is in England. The mourners carried pillows and blankets to defend against the cold while they shuffled along, hoping to get inside. The wind bespoke of snow. Orderly, somber, devoted Brits talked with pride of the man whose words were almost his only weapons. We readily abandoned our first plans and decided instead to rise early and claim a position as near to St. Paul's Cathedral as possible.

The next day, the sky was overcast, but the wind not quite so biting, as we staked our claim about a block from the site on the left side facing St. Paul's. The winding route was planned so the body would pass by landmarks closely related to Sir Winston Churchill's career.

London's Big Ben sounded at 9:45 a.m. Then it was silent the remainder of the day. The casket left Westminster Hall. Navy enlisted men drew the green carriage on foot. On it, the casket covered by the bright Union Jack, passed St. Margaret's Church where Samuel Pepys and John Milton were each married. All British military was in half step, the Regiment of the Household Guard wore splendid uniforms and black bearskin hats.

To the strains of Handel's "*Dead March*", the cortège entered first Parliament Street and on to Whitehall. Here stood hundreds of veterans from the European resistance, French, Belgians, Dutch, Danes, and Norwegians. Their survivors dipped their flags to the man whose voice had brought them hope. Next, the procession passed a house with two outside lights burning, No. 10 Downing St, passed the statue of Nelson in Trafalgar Square, up Fleet Street headed toward Ludgate Hill where we were fortunate to have front row positions not far from the massive cathedral. Everywhere one looked, there were people and more people all with one purpose—to honor their fallen hero, their protector.

The cortège carried the flag-wrapped casket up the narrow street—no more than five or six feet from us. Behind followed the veil-draped Lady Churchill and her daughter, Sarah. They were riding in the Queen's carriage on loan from the owners. The creeping carriage stopped immediately in front of us. We could easily have touched the carriage. It was that close. We were a block away from the cathedral.

St. Paul's, the Wrenn masterpiece, had survived all Nazi bombing attempts as if for this regal occasion. The huge door swung open and closed.

Those nearby on the steps had arrived the night before, fortified with blankets, pillows, and vacuum flasks of tea. Not expecting to get inside, they found comfort in being so near.

Churchill had helped arrange his own funeral under the code name, "Operation Hope Not" and all the music was glorious—not sad. The scripture, I Corinthians 15: 50-52:

> "*Now this I say, brethren, that flesh and*

blood cannot inherit the kingdom of God; neither doth corruption inherit incorruption.

Behold, I shew you a mystery; we shall not all sleep, but we shall all be changed. In a moment, in the twinkling of an eye, at the last trump; for the trumpet shall sound, and the dead shall be raised incorruptible, and we shall be changed."

According to the paper, everyone was there: representatives from more than 110 nations, which included six monarchs, five presidents, fifteen prime ministers, and many statesmen. They all joined in singing "The Battle Hymn of the Republic" written by an American composer but so fit for the occasion.

Interspersed were famous quotes from the leader's speeches in his voice:

"I have nothing to offer but blood, toil, tears, and sweat."

"So bear ourselves that if the British Empire and its Commonwealth last for 1,000 years man will say this was our finest hour."

"The General of the opposition told our Prime Minister, 'In three weeks we will wring your neck like a chicken.' "Some chicken...some neck!"*

General Eisenhower's tribute included:

"Here was a champion of freedom. May God grant that we and the generations to follow who will remember him, heed the lessons he taught

*us in his deeds, words, and life. May we carry
on his work until no nation lies in captivity, no
man is denied opportunity for fulfillment. Now
to you Sir Winston, my old friend, farewell."*

As the casket left the Cathedral, the honorary
pallbearers gave a last salute to the Old Warrior. Past
the Tower of London and the Tower Pier on the
Thames, the body was placed on a barge and then
transferred at Waterloo Station to a train waiting to take
the old soldier to Blenheim Cemetery.

Amid the pomp and pageantry, paperboys were
quietly dispensing special editions with headlines:
"Bend an Elbow for Old Winnie—His Request". The
mood was somber but dominated by love, admiration,
respect, worship, awe, and a sense of privilege to have
lived along beside him; a man who could save England
and Europe while Hitler was salivating to dominate
them. The country was united in pride for a man bigger
than the words he mastered. We were swept by the
orderly crowds into a nearby pub where we raised a
draft and reminisced about the man. Had his father,
rather than his mother been American, he might have
been an American citizen. At sixty-five, Churchill had
been considered a failure. With a command of words
and an iron will, however, he was the man that saved
England, the Western World, and Europe from Nazism.

Emily, I thought of you when I heard the music. It
was glorious.

Love,

Laurie

Chapter Four

Traveling and Shopping

 **Dear Emily,**

This was a shop-till-you-drop experience!

Some of my first trips were exploratory. There were cities not before visited by any A.M.C. merchants. Two trips to Brussels didn't warrant further visits. Cotton knits and a few sweaters did not compete. Brussels' lace-trimmed linens, their major export, were not popular at home.

The highlight of my second and last visit to Brussels was dinner at La Couronne, an elegant, small restaurant in a building dating to 1711 and located on the Grande Place. Three of us were seated at a front window overlooking the city square of impressive, gilded eighteenth century buildings that were probably four or five stories tall, punctuated by hand-crafted spires. To "gild the lily," a full moon added to the surreal splendor. The meal and the ambiance made this one of my most memorable restaurant experiences. In contrast was our meal on Rue de Boucham (Butcher's Street) the following evening.

Germany excelled in toys and Christmas decorations. Their fashion offerings were sturdy but drab and unappealing.

Marilyn Hartsell, Nancy Beatty, and Louise in Rome. Louise's reversible coat is llama from South America and is covering a matching plaid wool dress.

Amsterdam was not a destination for me but for international and continental flights. My plans to visit the Van Gogh Museum on a layover never materialized, but instead in 1975, my flight from Copenhagen to London was routed via Amsterdam. A huge banner announcing the "400th Anniversary of Vermeer" met me as I disembarked. An afternoon spent at the Rijks museum amid the largest assembled collection of Vermeer (only twenty-three pieces) was an unexpected treat. The museum was not crowded and only four or five pieces were shown in a single gallery. Most respected museums are proud to be owners of two or three pieces of the admired Flemish painter.

Two days in Lisbon failed to prove productive. I arrived with the name of the commissionaire, a telephone number, and the office address. After the first day of telephoning (before the day of the answering machine), I took a cab to the address but got no response. A commissionaire usually made himself available to any visitor who needed help in locating merchandise or services. Referrals were often made by a hotel concierge. We had read of the good values in handcrafted needlepoint rugs (before the day of business with China), and the concierge gave us the address of a store.

Our visit to the rug store was the highlight of our Lisbon stay. The shop showed probably 100 rugs in no more than five or six sizes. Many were copies of the French Savonnerie done in signature French coloring. After oohing and aahing over the find, the manager told us that the rugs were made by the women prisoners who were taught skills, furnished the patterns and materials, and paid fifty cents a day. The money accrued until the girls were released. They were able to buy the needed materials to go into business for themselves. Men were also taught skills most often in leather or wood, which meant that there were fewer repeat incarcerations. If a third world country (they used the term, not I) could accomplish this in the mid 1960s, why has the United States not been able to perfect a similar plan? I paid $200 for an eight-by-ten rug with burlap backing, and had it shipped for $20. I am still enjoying it in the guest bedroom.

I was told by management that when I was on vacation and saw saleable merchandise, I should purchase it, and the store would reimburse me for my time and expense. My address book carried information on A.M.C. offices and commissionaires from all over the world. Sometimes shopping proved more interesting than sightseeing. In Athens, where the telephone numbers for the commissionaires brought no response, I posted a letter given to me before I had left the United States for the daughter of a friend, and went on an island cruise. Upon returning to Athens, I found several telephone messages from a native. A Winston-Salem friend's daughter was married to the brother of Greece's Ambassador to the United States. The best specialty shop in Athens was owned by the same family. I was taken to the shop and introduced to much of the historic city that otherwise I would have missed. My lovely hotel overlooked Constitution Square where, at midnight, the place was so lively I felt as if the evening was only just beginning.

Assuming I might not return to the region, I had made reservations to visit Dubravnic. A friend had recently visited the seldom-mentioned attraction. The concierge at my Athens hotel failed to understand why I would elect to leave Athens for an unknown destination. According to him, I would regret it.

Under Tito, Dubravnic appeared to be a peace loving, quaint, not very prosperous city with fourteenth century walls. My hotel, the Excelsior, located in Old Town, had casement windows that opened onto a stone patio. Instead of sand, the strand was stone and covered with towels and chairs. Occasionally, a sunbather would dangle her feet into the water or else dive in and swim over to a projecting large stone and continue the sunbathing.

Food at the hotel was good, but unlike the Excelsior's in Italy. Fresh vegetables and fresh fruit were outstanding; fish and lamb appeared.

At night, the town erupted as throngs of natives walked down what seemed like a hundred stone steps to Plecon, the main street of the old city center. The space in front of Luza Square was the site of the summer festival where drama and music were paired against a backdrop of ancient churches, palaces and bell towers. The fourteenth century wall was built to secure Dubravnic from the Venetians and the Turks. Venetian influence is reflected in the buildings. Native costumes could be seen among the revelers as they promenaded and enjoyed fresh ice cream.

A day trip to Montenegro gave a different insight. A road had been carved through a solid rock mountain. For miles, the only vegetation was herbs growing between the rock ledges. Occasionally a tiny farmhouse would be seen on a small patch of soil that would support a family garden, a few fruit trees, a goat and a few chickens. Poverty and isolation made for a sad existence. Yugoslavia is the only country I have ever visited that I have found nothing to buy but a pretty picture book.

Back in Athens, I reclaimed the luggage left behind, repacked and caught a flight to Istanbul to investigate the hatred of the Greeks for the Turks. Many of the historic sites in Athens had suffered from the attacks by the Turks; the hatred was as if it had happened yesterday, not decades past.

Fields of blooming poppies, dilapidated old U.S.A. Plymouth cars, unpainted wooden houses (the only ones I had seen in any of my European travels) were my first impressions of Istanbul.

114

The commissionaire and his beautiful wife called for me at the Istanbul Hilton (I always preferred stopping at the fine native hotels but had been advised by travel agents that an American hotel was advisory here).

The young man and his lovely wife spoke perfect English and informed me that we would be dining at his private club, which was located on an isthmus, in the Bosphorus strait. Once there, all we could see was water everywhere. After I had enjoyed a delicious meal, my host told me that the tasty, tender meat was unborn calf. This was my only encounter with their most unusual meat. Back in the states, unborn calf purses, belts, and purse accessories were popular and not inexpensive.

This proved to be a profitable visit. Available were 100 percent Egyptian cloth tees made for specialty shops in Paris, cut and sewn cotton muslin tops decorated with matching color metal disks, color-block tees and tasteful stripes. The cotton tees led to a long profitable Turkey association with many of the other A.M.C. stores. The New York A.M.C. representative, Bernie Ozer, made a trip to Turkey and added it to the itinerary for traveling buyers. The young man who worked with me in Istanbul traveled to New York for seasonal meetings and to work with the buyers. The quality of the fabrics, skilled workmanship and European influence in the styling made the merchandise best sellers.

The time left was spent sightseeing; the sixth century Sophia, the Blue Mosque and Topkapi Palace, the Grand Bazaar (better known as the "thieves market"). Shopping here was unpleasant. If you dared to stop and admire an object, the shopkeeper would follow you as long as you were in the building and outside, which I found disgusting.

Without knowing what I was purchasing, I bought an entire box of antique, colorfully embroidered linen towels. They would make interesting gifts, I thought. My sister made pillow tops with the towels that I gave her, but it was not until a friend of hers who had lived in Middle East for years, identified them as Muslim wedding towels. *The Book Seller*, an Afghanistan novel, reinforced her story of the practice of stoning the bride to death on her wedding night if she failed to prove she was a virgin. The girls were taught at a young age to make the exquisite towels lavishly embroidered in red, green and purple yarn. Their appeal to me was lost.

One spring a friend and I spent a ten-day vacation in Spain prior to my business trip. At the Madrid airport while claiming our baggage, we spotted Henry Ford II and his current wife, Christina. From the front page of the *Herald Tribune,* we learned that Ford Motors was holding its annual European Dealers meeting in Madrid the following day. We had selected the same hotel—the Ritz.

Later that afternoon when I was getting a shampoo and blow-dry, I was seated adjacent to Christina. My eyes were drawn to a recent, red scar and a deep indention on the base of her neck—center front. It carried the markings of a tracheotomy that was too recent for plastic surgery.

Octavia and I decided to nurse a drink in the lobby while we waited for Mrs. Ford's exit that evening. Shortly after we were seated, a Spanish lady in her fifties was ushered in by her chauffeur. He took her coat to be hung. We scrutinized the lady in the black dress, diamond tiara, diamond necklace, bracelets, and numerous rings. About ten minutes later Christina arrived in a black wool dress with long sleeves and a turtleneck. Her only jewelry was a long strand of uncut emeralds. The two ladies embraced, the chauffeur was summoned by the desk clerk, and the three left. The señora wore a full-length black mink; Christina carried a triangle-fringed shawl of the same fabric as her dress. We enjoyed a laugh on the way to the flamenco club.

Emily, you would have loved the Christina / señora experience!

Love,

Laurie

Chapter Five

Life Beyond Work

 Dear Emily,

Lest you think that we did only work in Winston-Salem, there were afternoons in spring, summer, and fall, weekends, holidays, and vacation to play. A few minutes of gardening or jogging when in town kept me grounded.

I moved into a carriage house in Old Salem with a beautifully maintained garden and spent two years exploring the quaint 1760s Moravian village. In 1950 a group of influential citizens, some descendants of the founders, decided to rescue, preserve, and restore the unique landmark before it was lost forever. Today Old Salem Museum and Gardens consists of more than eighty acres, seventy historic buildings, restored or reconstructed, situated among acres of recreated gardens and landscaping.

One of my favorite entities is the Museum of Early Southern Decorative Arts, established and largely funded by Frank Horton and his mother who were antique collectors and authorities. The museum houses the finest collection of Southern furniture and decorative arts created before 1840. It exists due to a

118

statement heard by Mr. Horton at a symposium in Williamsburg. The speaker made the comment that no fine furniture or decorative arts had been produced in the South. That bold statement became a challenge to Mr. Horton and a lifelong pursuit.

Had he been living, Mr. Horton would have felt vindicated in January 2007 when MESDA presented the loan exhibition at the 53rd Annual Winter Antique Show at the Seventh Regiment Armory, Park Avenue, New York City. The magazine, *Antiques*, for the same month gave the cover and feature section to the collections of MESDA. It is generally conceded that the pottery collection ranks among the best in the nation. Winston-Salem is proud to be the home of our country's most authentic, historical restoration. Today tourists and scholars from all over the world are enjoying Mr. Horton's collections and research.

Golf was never intended for merchants. There was just not enough time. Also, then woman were not allowed on many courses on Saturdays or Sundays. That didn't prevent me from having lots of golfing friends and following many of the member/guest tournaments at North Carolina clubs. The annual Firestone Tournament played on the Donald Ross No. 2 at Pinehurst as well as the Steeplechase at Southern Pines were priorities.

The Blue Ridge Parkway is little more than an hour away and encouraged many day trips with picnic lunches; time to enjoy the wild flowers and spectacular scenery. Today a day trip most often means a visit to a sophisticated winery and a gourmet meal.

Summer vacations meant as little exertion as possible—no travel. For many summers, I vacationed with my sister and her husband at North Litchfield Beach, a small, quiet, private strand, sheltered by forest on either end. It was located near Pauley's Island, known for its Hammock Shop, garden shops, and a Lilly Boutique. Ten minutes down 201 South was interesting Georgetown with historic houses, remains of once charming rice plantations and much-used elite hunting lodges. Ted Turner is a large landholder there.

Every afternoon at about 5 p.m., the shrimp boats would arrive and offer for sale the freshest, best-tasting shrimp ever. Buying and preparing a week's supply of boiled shrimp was a ritual. We would return and prepare frozen shrimp to bring home.

About one hour south of Litchfield, is fabulous Charleston where we always spent a day browsing the fine antique shops, the boutiques, the garden shops and lunching in the walled courtyard of the Mills House.

One calm morning on the beach at North Litchfield has remained visually in my mind all these years. The three of us were sunning on the beach near our house at about 11 a.m. when my brother-in-law saw a swimmer some distance out, go under once, come up and go under again. Charles asked if there was a good swimmer available, adding that he was a smoker. After no response, Charlie immediately swam out and located the 275 – 300 pound body of an older man. He dragged him to the shore, turned him over and pumped out the water. Then, he proceeded to perform mouth-to-mouth resuscitation while pumping his rib cage. He asked one of the many on-lookers to call an ambulance and to advise his family in the house almost directly behind us.

The ambulance arrived shortly and claimed the body. The family never came to the scene; neither did they come to our house next door to thank the rescuer. The doctor who retrieved the body believed the swimmer had suffered a coronary; he died suddenly. A media gal I knew from Winston-Salem composed a ballad about the strange scene. It was as if the family would have preferred the victim be buried at sea. I understand there is a delay in moving a body from one state to another. The family next door came and went as if nothing had happened. The automobile with the Illinois plate was still there when we left.

Between my annual trips to Europe, frequent New York market trips, numerous overnight trips to Richmond, annual A.M.C. meetings hosted by member stores all over the United States, trips to all twelve North Carolina stores, plus two stores in Danville, Virginia, there was little idle time. Two of my neighbors tried to make my life more interesting—so they seemed to think. A prominent banker lived diagonally across the street from me. After burying his wife of many years, he asked me to select some clothes for his two teenage daughters. Soon he was arriving at my front door with two gin and tonics before dinner. After he found that he knew my family, he suggested we get married, move into his larger house and rent mine. He added that he knew I liked the neighborhood, and he had a view of the sixth hole on the golf course. I countered that I enjoyed my work too much to stay home. He said my problem was that I didn't need a meal ticket. Women were calling him continuously.

He was scheduled for an exploratory operation on his throat while I was to be away. A month later, I picked up a fruit basket and stopped in to see him to find that the biopsy had proved malignant. He had had the cancer operation and had brought his nurse home with him. They were married as soon as he was able and planned a European honeymoon. When he went for his final checkup, he was told that the cancer had returned. His condition declined rapidly thereafter. The new wife wasted no time in getting a revised will written that favored her over his two daughters who no longer lived at home. She refused to let his banking friends of thirty years visit him. They were met midway between their cars and the house. Outgoing and jovial, he had many cherished friends who wanted to see him to talk and visit. She made his life miserable under the picture of "protection."

The new bride got the lovely house and furnishings. The girls were distraught that they were allowed none of their mother's personal belongings. Months later, the widow was diagnosed with Parkinson's disease and moved into a care facility.

One Sunday afternoon I was packing for a 5 p.m. flight to New York when my doorbell rang. At the door was my backyard neighbor in a dark suit. I was accustomed to seeing him in his gardening garb while exchanging gardening tips over the ivy-covered back fence. A recently retired engineer with Western Electric, he spent his spare time lecturing at luncheon meetings of the Rotary, Kiwanis, or Lions Clubs on the benefits of growing organic vegetables and saving the environment by eliminating pesticides and cutting back on fertilizer. In the seventies, he was a man ahead of his time. After one of the downtown luncheon meetings, he would stop by my office for a quick report. My secretary had suspected an interest, but I had dismissed the idea completely as absurd.

After asking Mr. "C" in, I told him my schedule and that I could spare only a few minutes. He sat down and immediately told me that his wife of forty-plus years (I had never seen her) was in a local hospital with a terminal illness. He wanted me to know that he had never lived alone and wanted to ask me to marry him in due time. I was so taken aback by this inhumane action that I lost my speech. Finally I said, "Mr. "C", I have enjoyed exchanging gardening tips with you, appreciated the fresh vegetables you shared, but couldn't we just remain friends?" Then he asked if he could put a gate in my back fence to avoid having to walk around the block. This was my opening. "Good fences make good neighbors," I said. He left, hat in hand, urging me to give it serious thought.

The following Saturday morning, my next-door neighbor advised me that Mr. "C" buried his wife on Thursday and accompanied his son home to Maryland on Friday.

Meanwhile, the widow's bridge club at Western Electric was making plans to corral Mr. "C". He was invited to eat and play bridge with the widows of his deceased friends. Several months later, he married the widow of a former co-worker, and she moved into his house.

We continued to garden over the fence and everyone seemed happy with the arrangement. After a few months, he admitted that he had married a woman to take care of him, not vice versa. She needed care, so he was putting his unconventional engineer-planned house on the market and moving to Arizona where his wife's son lived. Several years later, we learned that neither he nor his wife was still living.

After I moved to Winston-Salem, I visited the Moravian Church with an open mind, but I joined the downtown Presbyterian Church. There were no groups for professional singles, and I met few people.

I also routinely attended church in New York at the 5th Avenue Presbyterian Church. There, I met many interesting people at the coffee hour following the 11 a.m. service. Occasionally, a New York friend and I would attend a mid-week lecture there. Dr. Kirkland was the able minister there for years. He was followed by Dr. Maurice Boyd, another jewel.

In 1967, Barbara Babcock Lassiter opened the expansive Winston-Salem home of her grandfather, R. J. Reynolds, the tobacco magnet, to the public. With the guidance of Thomas Hoving, she and her father assembled the foundation for a fine American painting collection. Their timing was perfect. They purchased prime paintings that are unapproachable today. Paintings by Thomas Cole, Worthington Whittridge, Asher B. Durand, Albert Bierstadt, Frederick Church, Jasper Cropsey, and Martin Johnson Heade, are representative of the major American artists to be found in comparable museums. Acquisitions are constantly made, and it remains one of America's finest home museums. Reynolda House is beautifully located on many acres of lawn, forest and gardens, adjacent to Reynolda Village where the shops are found in a former barn, silo, stables, blacksmiths' shop, and other supporting dependencies. The original estate consisted of more than 1000 acres. Reynolda House, with Ms. Babcock as director, was responsible for bringing many of the represented artists to Winston-Salem to lecture and to meet the supporters. A few of the artists I was privileged to meet and hear lecture were Jacob Laurence, Audrey Flack, and numerous art scholars. Thomas Hoving flew his plane down for a special event.

The director planned educational trips to the homes and communities in which the artists had lived. I was fortunate to have been able to join a group on the Hudson River Tour, the Concord, Massachusetts Tour, the Jasper Cropsey Studio, and the home of his niece who shared her major collection of his work in her Greenwich, Connecticut residence. Mary Reynolds, a daughter who grew up in Reynolda House, had us for lunch at her Greenwich estate.

The collection constantly expands. In 2005, an educational building was added which provided a large gallery for highlighting its own collections and for traveling shows, lectures, and musicals. To guarantee its survival, in 2002, Reynolda House became a part of Wake Forest University. Reynolda House remains one of the area's finest institutions.

In the 1960s, on the other side of town, the North Carolina School of the Arts was established. The story goes that the site for our arts school was open for bids and the movers and shakers in Winston-Salem raised $2 million the first day before lunch and were able to laud it over its Charlotte rival. Earlier Philip Hanes had organized the first Arts Council (nationally) in Winston-Salem. Later he was asked to help organize the National Arts Council in Washington, D. C.

The school here continued to expand and improve its status. The University of North Carolina School of the Arts is the first state public art school in the nation. Our citizens are blessed with music, drama, dance, and movies that few cities the size of Winston-Salem can match. The school makes great contributions to the local symphony, opera, ballet, and church choirs by participating professors and students. Many of the school's productions compare favorably with Broadway shows. "West Side Story," presented in 2007, was directed by the same Gerald Freedman that assisted Jerome Robbins in the original musical in New York in 1957. Chancellor John Manceri, Ethan Steifel, soon to be Dean of Dance, and Dean Jordan Kerns, a well-known Los Angeles producer who headed the School of Filmmaking, are all examples of the tops in their respective fields and attract others who excel in the arts.

Graduates of the School are highly recognized in

their fields: music, drama, dance, film, directing, costume and set design. Alumni are recognized anywhere the arts thrive. In earlier days, Rosemary Harris, a local actress, directed a production each spring. Her daughter, Jennifer Ehle, is following in her mother's footsteps as an outstanding actress. You will often see alumni receiving awards at the Oscars and Emmys.

Life after hours in New York offered a completely different picture than evenings in Winston-Salem. In New York, there was never an idle moment during the market openings in the fall and spring. Fashion shows by Jeffery Beene, Bill Blass, Halston, Oscar de la Renta, and Larry Aldrich attracted many celebrities, society gals, and the press—always "W" from Women's Wear Daily. Calvin Klein was the first to take his show to a loft in the Village before lofts were "cool". Many shows become major productions.

Liz Claiborne staged a big party each fall until the events outgrew each location. Enormous amounts of people, strobe lights, loud music, and heavy smoke each year brought an end to the tradition of parties hosted by Liz Claiborne.

Estee Lauder invited a Thalhimer table each January to the "Ship of Hope" charity ball held at the Waldorf with all proceeds going to Jewish charities. It was a beautiful affair.

One of my favorites was the Hanes Hosiery party each spring. For years, it was dinner at Club 21. After outgrowing that space, the party became a cocktail dance at the Hotel Pierre. A great band, open bar, and plenty of floor space attracted so many uninvited guests that it had to be discontinued. Gordon and Copey Hanes were on hand for a gracious "good night" to their guests. It was a great party. I have a fond memory of the president of Higbees asking me to dance. He was of Scandinavian descent and a grand dancer. Before I knew what happened, he was guiding me through the rumba, the samba, the mambo, and some dances I no longer remember. Other dancers moved off the floor, and we were doing a solo for hundreds of on-lookers. Luckily, he was an excellent dancer and a strong leader.

My friendship with a market representative over the years resulted in my invitation to a fabulous wedding in Washington, D.C. in the spring of 1969. The date coincided with my return from Europe, and was to be held at the Shoreland Hotel where Elizabeth Taylor was married the prior Saturday. (I can't come up with which number husband it was.) Arrangements were made with Evelyn Sosnik, the capable French Room buyer, to have my party clothes sent to the hotel.

My noon flight from London arrived at Kennedy at 3 p.m., Friday, on time. A New York friend, also invited, met me at the airport. We drove to Washington and arrived at the Shoreland in time for the get-acquainted cocktail hour.

Saturday was a full day starting with a gourmet buffet lunch. There was stuffed pig and pheasant displayed, along with carved ice figures and plenty of champagne. This lovely event set the tone for the beautiful day.

The 2 p.m. wedding was held in an adjoining room decorated with pink flowers and an arbor of pink roses, where the bride and groom exchanged vows. The ceremony was completed by the smashing of the wine glass. They were a beaming handsome pair leaving the room.

At 7 p.m., the newlyweds and approximately 200

guests dressed to their nines were seated in a private dining room for the reception dinner/dance. Beautifully appointed tables with spectacular flower arrangements, favors and scores of wine glasses prepared the guests for the outstanding meal that followed. Ambiance, food, service, music, and friends assured a happy occasion. Music was provided by one of the New York debutant bands. There was plenty of space for dancing. At 1 a.m., the parents of the bride (of the Mars Candy family) said good night to each guest. Martha Stewart would have difficulty topping this wedding.

My introduction to the wild animal theme, other than in the up-scale magazines, was at a party in the sixties at Diane Von Furstenberg's apartment overlooking 5th Avenue. A leopard rug greeted us as we stepped off the elevator on her floor. Her bedroom was animal all the way. I recall that her bed was turned back which was unusual then. Her signature wrap dress was a bestseller in all the jungle prints. In 2001, it made a roaring return to 7th Avenue.

I regretted missing a party at Gloria Vanderbilt's apartment. My friend said that almost everything was executed in collage. Once or twice, I did see Ms. Vanderbilt in the showroom where her jeans were shown. She was petite, more so than her photographs reflected and very pretty. Her pale make-up reminded me of the native Japanese women.

One of our manufacturers of upscale children's clothing had a box at Lincoln Center, which he generously shared with his customers.

My favorite evenings in New York included dinner at a good Upper East Side restaurant, outstanding food, good conversation and a stop by the Carlyle to enjoy

Bobby Short at the piano. Other evenings might be a pre-theatre dinner followed by a Broadway play or a performance at Lincoln Center and a visit to the Russian Tea Room.

Emily, I admit I do miss the fine restaurants and museums.

Love,

Laurie

Chapter Six

New Horizon—The Orient

Dear Emily,

Off to the Orient, a whole other world to explore!

Early fall of 1976, I joined five people from A.M.C. stores on an exploratory trip to the Far East. Prices had advanced in Europe due to the prosperity and demand on the continent and from Japan. We no longer received priority on shipping. In addition, much of the sportswear we were buying in New York was coming from Hong Kong: McMullen, Marisa Christina, and David Crystal were heavy importers from the Orient. Each of us had European importing experience. Sue, from Higbees, and I represented the female viewpoint.

We arrived at our high-tech Pan Pacific Hotel in Tokyo at about 9 p.m. After checking in, we agreed to meet in the bar for a light snack where our hamburgers turned out to be soy burgers, a first for each of us. The bedside wall and one bathroom wall reminded me of the dashboard of a plane; never had I seen so much technology in a hotel.

The next morning our cabbie located the A.M.C. office where we met the manager and the sportswear representatives. The samples they showed were made of quality material and were well tailored but the limited offerings showed that they were not yet ready for exporting to our stores. Several years later they had developed a handsome collection of velveteen blazers in ten colors that we and other A.M.C. stores ordered by the thousands.

Management in our hotel insisted we carry at all times a card and map showing the name and location of the Pan Pacific Hotel. It was not unusual for a guest to get lost. Cabbies didn't know all sections of the huge city. The bullet train was a new experience if you didn't mind being twice as crowded as in the New York subway.

Saturday morning, we shopped the large, crowded department store, Mitsukoshi. Prices were shocking when compared with ours. We were impressed by the department of fine dolls. It was customary for each girl to receive a beautiful doll ($200 and up) for each birthday until she was an adult. (Remember there was one child per family.) Kimonos were created in beautiful patterned silks and sold for four figures. Obis were priced in the hundreds. I surmised that since few people in Tokyo owned houses or automobiles, they enjoyed spending money on expensive clothes, art, and jewelry. Japanese women are the prettiest of the Orientals.

Food in Tokyo was good but spare; we always left a restaurant hungry. The office manager suggested a steak. I was amazed when my plate arrived with a steak that could not have been more than three ounces plus a few decorative veggies. A fruit stand supported our survival.

When we arrived at the Hong Kong Airport, we were met by a stretch Mercedes limo that transported us to the Peninsula Hotel, an English hotel. The houseboys who took charge of our hand luggage, the fresh flowers and fresh fruit in the lovely room told me I would love the place. In the lobby and house restaurants, we were surrounded by fellow Americans, familiar faces from 7th Avenue.

I was awakened the next morning by a strange noise that sounded like people walking through dead leaves. A rush to the window overlooking Nathan Road showed hundreds of young Chinese all dressed in dark Mao pantsuits, shuffling along in their thongs. This accounted for the scraping noise. Short, all less than five feet, the thick black hair, all cut the same; it was impossible to determine the sex. More than all I had read or seen in pictures, this spoke of "Communism". There were no distinguishing characteristics, no personalities, no individuality, no laughter—the masses subservient to The Leader. I knew I was witnessing another time and place. Never have I felt happier to be an American.

It was Saturday morning. With no work, throngs of people had taken over the walking street for an outing of sightseeing. There was no money to spend. The Star Ferry docked less than two blocks away and had funneled hundreds of non-descript Chinese workers into Nathan Road which was their 5th Avenue. I shall remember to tell you what Nathan Road looked like ten years later in 1986.

For once, I realized that I was witnessing a really different culture. The shipping schedule, which was pushed under my door each morning by Sea-Land, a subsidiary of Reynolds Tobacco, helped me feel connected to home.

The A.M.C. office on Nathan Road consisted of a manager and several English-speaking helpers. Our first stop was a factory nearby where teenage boys were each operating as many as six large knitting machines clearly marked: "Made in PA, U.S.A.". (They were identical to the computerized machines our mills owned. Our machines were forced to idle when the unions objected to the elimination of jobs.) We observed hundreds of Fair-Isle sweaters being knitted. If a thread broke or a pattern malfunctioned, the machine shut down. We visited a showroom where hundreds of handmade knit sweaters were shown; others were displayed in our A.M.C. office.

Louise and Ervin Schiff from the Richmond Thalhimers store at the Verandah, Repulse Bay, Hong Kong, 1978

We had been buying certain Hong Kong items through our New York office, so we were familiar with some of the resources. However, we met few, if any, of the principals of the resources. Maybe they didn't speak English, or maybe they lived in what we then referred to as "Red China". There was just no way all the merchandise offered could have been produced in Hong Kong, as it was labeled. The standard of living between the residents of the British Colony and mainland China were eons apart. The United States had no trading relations with China until twelve years after our first visit to Hong Kong.

The teen-aged boys who ran the knitting machines in Hong Kong made about a dollar a day; hand knitters in Korea were making fifty cents per day plus room and board in a dormitory while the unions in the States were fighting to increase the hourly wages from $12.50 an hour to $15 an hour. There is no putting the toothpaste back into the tube, but I do believe that the unions hastened the rush to the Orient. If we, the merchants, did not pursue the opportunity, our New York manufacturers would, and we would pay the cost of the middleman. In fact, a New York/Pennsylvania sweater man asked me what I was doing in Hong Kong. "Don't you know this is our territory," he proclaimed. Not many years later, there were no sweater makers in the States. Either they went out of business, or they went to the Orient. What started as a small trend has spread into a phenomenon that has created a global economy. It was probably inevitable, but as I look back, it is difficult not to regret that I contributed to a process that has taken all the excitement out of retailing.

When I started my annual trips to Europe in the early sixties, only wealthy people went to Europe. Only Baptist missionaries had been to China. The change was gradual but constant.

One of our New York manufacturers introduced us to one of the finest restaurants in the world, Gaddy's. Located on the street floor of the Peninsula Hotel, both the hotel and the restaurant were five stars. I had some difficulty with the native food, although the men in our group loved the "hundred-year-old eggs" and the local brew. When in doubt, go continental, was my motto.

Reluctantly, we left the luxurious hotel with its many fine restaurants and European designer shops for Taipei in Taiwan. Here we stopped at the Palace, an enormous red Chinese pagoda built by Chang Kai-shek, the President of China from 1948-49, as his new home when he was ousted from the mainland.

The Palace was built to accommodate more than sixty family members and supporting staff. There were also several dependencies in the back. I don't know what renovations were made when it was converted to a hotel, but we were told that many of the original furnishings remained in the public rooms.

As soon as I had an opportunity, I asked about the National Taiwan Museum and was assured that a visit was on our itinerary. A friend, who had recently visited Taipei, had assured me that this was the finest collection of Oriental art in existence. While Chang Kai-shek was planning his new home and furnishings, he was also making arrangements to have all the mainland fine art flown to Taipei for preservation. A friend was in China with the Flying Tigers at the time, and he said it was a superbly planned and executed operation. He believed that Chang Kai-shek had the maneuvers so well organized that twenty planes loaded and flew all the treasures to Taipei one moonless night while Mao was hidden in the hills planning his next move.

Hitler had plotted and carried out his first invasion to benefit his private art collection. He had a well-researched list of all the finest privately owned art collections in Europe in the late thirties and early forties. The wealthy Jewish families in Poland, then in France, were his prime targets for the prison camps. Worth noting is the fact that one of Hitler's top henchmen diverted some of the best pieces to his own hunting lodge.

A friend in Winston-Salem had grown up in Brazil as the child of missionaries and had a friend who became the tutor to Kai-shek's children in Peking (now Beijing). Missionaries no longer felt safe and were returned to the States. In the seventies, Gertrude visited her friend at the Palace in Taipei and insisted I not fail to see certain items in the collection at the National Museum. After not seeing any of the "must-sees" on my list, I asked our guide if I could have overlooked them. The guide laughed heartily and quickly explained that if exhibits were changed twice a year, more than twenty-five years would be required to display all the treasures buried in these hills! I was seeing less than 1/50th of the cache. Is it any wonder that China refuses to recognize the Republic of Taiwan?

The perception, planning, and execution of a plot to save Chinese antiques from our earliest civilization, proved a priceless gift to the world. Would they have gone the way of all the books—bonfire?

It seemed that most people in Taipei spoke English. The United States had kept a military base there for years, and we sensed a feeling of appreciation and respect. Their standard of living far exceeded that of Hong Kong and Korea and reflected in their pricing of merchandise. Many small cars and motor bikes were seen on the streets as opposed to only bicycles at our previous stop. At the time, their chief export was electronics. A "made in Taiwan" label stood for exceptional quality control and dependable products. Even today, I would put their wares more on a par with

Japan—far above those made in China.

We found well-styled machine-knit sweaters that became best sellers. Elk skin purses and purse accessories were priced well and desirable. With the dominance of China in all textiles and clothing, the resourceful, industrious, dedicated workers no doubt have found their niche in technology.

From Taipei, we took a small smoke-filled plane to Seoul, South Korea. The fact that every native lit a cigarette was a sign of prosperity in Taiwan, but suffocating for those who didn't smoke. We registered at the Chosen, supposedly the best hotel in town.

The following day we visited a warehouse where rural girls lived in a nearby dormitory and produced hand-knit sweaters in the drafty warehouse/factory. Most knitters sat at tables; some on floors. They made fifty cents a day plus room and board. When possible the girls would walk home on weekends to share their earnings with their needy families. As depressing as it appeared, no doubt both parties benefited from the small wages. As they expanded their products, the Koreans became dependable and profitable resources. We visited several startup businesses that were not prepared for exporting; their enthusiasm was more developed than their product.

We were amazed to find almost any current fiction offered in paperbacks for fifty cents each, which was a favorite with travelers.

Food was so-so, non-memorable. After a frightening experience in my room, I was ready to visit the notorious gambling casino. I was to meet my fellow travelers in the hotel lobby at 6:30 p.m. As I attempted to leave my room, the doorknob and all attachments fell on the floor at my feet, everything except the outside knob. After calling the clerk to leave a message for my friends, I explained my predicament to the desk clerk. Soon a young boy arrived yelling: "open, now", followed by "stupid, stupid". After again speaking with management, the young boy, secured by a rope, entered the adjoining room and hand-walked on the ledge to my window, entered and lifted the door off the hinges for my escape. Could not the hinges have been lifted from the outside? When I returned later that night, everything was in order.

This was my only time to gamble at a casino, Paradise Hill, I believe. As we entered the large dimly lit and smoky room, two men stood up and called my name. They were the owners of a large moderately priced sweater house in New York and in 1976 were looking for a factory to transfer their Pennsylvania production. They asked me to join them at Black Jack. We were winning and having fun when, at 10:30 p.m., a voice on the loudspeaker announced an 11 p.m. curfew in English. No private cars or cabs would be tolerated on the streets after that time, which meant we either left at 10:30 p.m. or spent the night at the busy casino. My group immediately left for our hotel, while my friends elected to play through the night.

Seoul seemed impoverished until we drove through a large, impressive Government Plaza several miles from downtown. With a vision like that, one felt encouraged about a future we could not have predicted. In recent years, I have seen this plaza on television several times. When the Olympics were there in 1988 it seemed that the forward-looking plaza was the hub of a prosperous South Korea. The Koreans impressed us as determined, dedicated people who were smart enough to zero in on lower-priced electronics as Taiwan prices escalated. Not until ten years after the exploratory trip did I visit the missing link in the Far East—mainland China.

Management at A.M.C. New York, decided the time had come to move the annual Far East Sportswear meeting from San Francisco (point of entry for samples) to Hong Kong. Offices in Tokyo, Taipei and Seoul reported to the Hong Kong office.

For ten or twelve years, these meetings were attended by as many as one hundred buyers and merchandisers each year. Large amounts of money were spent for sweaters, jackets, blouses, skirts, and slacks. Quality control assured us of good products. A.M.C. was the groundbreaker and made a large presence in the Orient long before China opened its doors to world trade. Christmas decoration buyers arrived several years later and stayed longer than the sportswear buyers. They copied many expensive German ornaments.

With the advancement of technology, the rising cost of travel, and the move of New York manufacturers to China, the importance of the meetings became compromised. The shift in ownership of A.M.C. stores could and did change overnight. These meetings served their purpose well in their time.

Emily, on this trip to Tokyo, Hong Kong, Taipei, and Seoul I was disappointed not to find any historical sites. All there was to do was eat and shop. So unlike Europe!

Love,

Lauren

Chapter Seven

Sell or Be Acquired?

*1954 Thalhimers in downtown Winston-Salem, NC.
The building was formerly Sosnik's.*

Dear Emily,

This was a shocker! I could be moving to Richmond, Virginia where you are. Let me tell you what happened.

Just as we felt we were getting our Winston-Salem stores headed in the right direction, the manager of the Thalhimers store in Greensboro retired and the two buying teams were combined.

In 1959 Thalhimers, North Carolina, existed in name only with a volume of $1 million (my Junior Department at Ivey's did half that). Twenty years later, there were three stores in Winston-Salem, followed by stores in Greensboro, Durham, Raleigh, Fayetteville, and High Point, that had a volume of over sixty million. New stores averaged 130,000 to 180,000 square feet. Total Corporation had grown from twenty million to 160 million.

Covering twelve North Carolina stores plus two Danville, Virginia, stores required good buyers and assistants, strong department managers, dedicated sales personnel, and lots of travel. Buyers were expected to visit each store once a month when possible. This meant leaving town early and returning late. When a new store opened, we were in the respective cities four nights. Demographics played an important role in the assortments and contributed highly to our success.

When John Christian, Jr., General Merchandise Manager of the Richmond Division, accepted a position with the May Company in Akron, Ohio, Sherwood Michael replaced him in 1969. Dick Ayscue of the Danville, Virginia store moved to Winston-Salem as General Manager of the North Carolina Division. His responsibilities were properties, personnel, and payroll. I continued to be responsible for merchandising and sales, display, advertising, and bottom line. We each reported to Richmond.

From the mid-sixties until the mid-eighties, the department stores in this country grew at a rate never witnessed before or since. Malls and shopping centers were being announced relentlessly. Merchants felt self-pressured not to be left out.

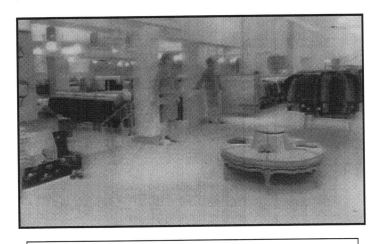

Salem Shop Downtown Winston Salem Store 1956

It was in this climate of expansion that storeowners realized they had everything at stake! They had to either keep expanding or be taken over by an aggressor. Rich's and Neiman-Marcus had each elected to pick their partners rather than be subjected to an unfriendly takeover. The Thalhimer brothers knew that they owned a good franchise of loyal customers but didn't feel like risking what they had accomplished by over-extending. Allied had made an overture—frightening. The brothers

knew the move made by Neiman-Marcus and the
outward signs of success and were open to discussion
with Carter Hawley Hale, Neiman-Marcus' white
knight.

*Friendly Center Store, Greensboro, North
Carolina. Photo courtesy of Thalhimers archive.*

Negotiations were a well-kept secret, and it came
as a total shock when Mr. William Thalhimer, Jr. came
to Winston-Salem in the spring of 1978 and announced
that the Company had been sold to Carter Hawley Hale.
Not one of us had ever heard of the West Coast
Company headquartered in Los Angeles, and we had
often done business in the city! We were assured that
nothing would change, everything would remain the

same. Our stores would have complete autonomy!

Richmond and North Carolina were separate divisions. There were two sets of operating records. The many service departments in the large downtown Richmond store took a toll on its net profit. Although we were prorated a fee for parent services, we showed a higher net profit. From the beginning, the North Carolina division had the higher unit sales. Soon it was showing a higher gross margin percentage. As volume grew, the North Carolina branch showed the larger dollar contribution. I was crushed when told that it didn't make sense for Carter Hawley Hale to have two Thalhimer stores reporting when they already had eight or ten separate divisions. This meant moving to Richmond, taking early retirement, or taking another job. I was allowed to remain in Winston-Salem for another year during consolidation.

Twenty fleeting, full, happy years had passed and again I faced a change I didn't seek. It was time to reminisce, recall and record.

Although with my new undertaking, it was difficult not to feel deprived with no history, little experienced help, and few systems; it proved to be a positive. Mr. Michael, Mr. Charles, the new team and I were able to chart our own course. Usually this privilege is reserved for the owner. Since the only customer loyalty we inherited was from Sosnik's French Room, and since my experience at Ivey's had been with better merchandise, it was not difficult to decide to target the better customer. Limited square footage in our first store forced us to make classification choices. As we opened larger stores, we expanded our offerings.

Evelyn Sosnik had made many market trips with the former owner, knew most of the manufacturers and the French Room customers. She developed a designer business not enjoyed by any other department store in the two Carolinas. Most of the couture business in our area was done by fine specialty stores. Montaldo's owned the largest share. Lillian Montaldo had supported the high-end market through World War II; else many resources would not have survived. We were not recognized by all suppliers for several seasons but we didn't give up. We were later able to buy from every house on 7th Avenue, but did promise several top houses not to advertise their merchandise or show it in our windows—with respect to Ms. Montaldo.

Crabtree Mall store in Raleigh, North Carolina—
Photo courtesy of Thalhimers Archives.

We had three professional sales associates who wrote tremendous books from some of the top lines: Bill Blass, Jeffrey Beene, Teal Trainer, Pauline Trigere, Cecil Chapman, Oscar de la Renta, Gloria Sachs, Maurice Retner, Adele Simpson, St. John Knits,

Davidow suits, Goldstein coats, and Originala Coats. In Designer Sportswear, you would find Blassport, Ann Klein, Calvin Klein, and Betty Hansen.

We had a strong Better Sportswear department with excellent buyers and superb sales associates. Some of the lines carried were Kimberly Knits, Blyley Knits, Lilly, McMullen, Hadley, David Crystal, Pendleton, Perry Ellis, Ralph Lauren, Jones of New York, Liz Claiborne, and we sold our share of Villager, John Meyer, and J. G. Hook and tons of cashmere sweaters. European imports contributed to exciting, different and interesting assortments. Our swimwear manufacturers said we enjoyed one of the strongest, more profitable operations.

Staff Photo by Cookie Snyder

Robert Weatherman (second from left) accepts keys from Sherwood Michael as Charles Thalhimer and Miss Louise Thomas look on.

New Thalhimer Store Opens Here

We enjoyed good business in moderate dresses, junior dresses and junior sportswear, shoes, handbags, costume jewelry, hosiery, blouses, and a highly developed cosmetics department made a lively street floor. Quality lines were well received in Lingerie and Children's departments. Fine china, silver, crystal and fine linens were popular. Men's clothing was a business already owned by long-entrenched merchants. We concentrated on men's furnishings.

We never reached the goals I aspired for, but we attempted to present well-selected assortments geared to the demographics and offered special services. We moved broken assortments for consolidation, took special orders, delivered the customer's purchases to her home—a luxury we had to discontinue. Our profit margin was credible. We had caring, courteous, knowledgeable sales assistants. They knew their customers' preferences and called them when new merchandise arrived.

We had capable fitters and seamstresses who could and did perform miracles. I recall a customer who would order two blouses and two skirts in size sixteen and have a dress made in her size.

Multiple stores in six North Carolina cities plus Danville, Virginia required a strong back-up team responsible for marking, transportation, properties, security, payroll, and personnel. First Sherwood Michael, followed by Dick Ayscue, coordinated the store operations. The branch store managers reported to these area managers. Their astute cost controls meant that profits flowed to the bottom line.

Emily, shoppers today, under age thirty, may think I'm hallucinating. As you know, in the larger cities, Saturdays were special: to spend the morning shopping at Wanamakers, Rich's, or Marshall Field's. Lunch in the tearoom was highlighted by an organ recital. The afternoons could be spent exploring galleries of fine art and collections from around the world. The fine department stores that arrived to cultivate good taste peaked in America in the mid-twentieth Century and crashed twenty to thirty years later. Present and future generations have been cheated of a grand experience.

Love,

Louise

Sherwood Michael, Louise Thomas, and Bruce Crawford, Advertising Director—Parkway Plaza store opening, 1966

Part Four:

Then to Richmond, Virginia

Downtown Winston-Salem window displays by Allen Blackford, 1960s.

Chapter One

Settling In

 Dear Emily,

Moving to Richmond was easier than I anticipated. It was a new, young, friendly neighborhood.

After looking at older houses on Monument Avenue and Windsor Farms, I was discouraged. All houses visited needed new kitchens and new bathrooms. I had neither the time and patience, nor the connections to undertake such a daunting task. Finally, I found a house I liked under construction off Pump Road. I should have rented and bought an adjacent farm that is now near one of the South's largest shopping centers— Pump Road Shopping Center.

The architect/builder was easy to work with and made changes to meet my needs—raised paneled cabinets and bookshelves for my library. The wide mullioned tall windows set the tone for my antique furniture. Shutters were fitted and painted to match the contrasting trim throughout the house.

The move and transition were easier than expected. The house was bright, airy, and comfortable, though smaller than the house I left behind. The silk draperies went into storage, a few swags and cornices were installed. A small dependency in the backyard was of the same Williamsburg style as the house and held my gardening tools. The wooded backyard was fenced, and boxwoods followed the oval pattern of the back lawn.

I decided to rent my house in Winston-Salem, but I soon regretted the decision. My first tenants were an interim college president and his wife, who had always lived in college housing. The wife called incessantly, asking how to turn on the air conditioning, what to do with a piece of poison ivy found in a flower border, what to do with a can of paint left in a pantry. I was paged in a New York showroom for the last request. My first thought was that my house was on fire. Other tenants were an improvement, but the first one convinced me that I was not intended to be a "landlady." Fortunately, I was able to take the cost of repairs off my taxes.

My first day in a new setting was mid-March 1979—twenty years, to the day, after joining the company in 1959 in Winston-Salem. It was déjà-vu. All buyers, assistants, and merchandisers from the fashion departments were in the basement of the downtown Richmond store preparing for a "Down from Up Sale."

Last-season fashion merchandise had been transferred from the four suburban stores to the anchor store for final clearance. The selections consisted of fall and holiday merchandise that had been cleared in North Carolina stores in season. Heavy, dark woolens and holiday attire were no bargain at half price in mid-March. That day we realized that our job would not be without problems—a mindset. The merchant responsible for the disaster was promoted!

Many of our top resources in North Carolina were not represented in the Richmond stocks. Little could be done to stimulate spring/summer sales, but there was time to implement a new plan, a new look for fall. Year-end showed a sizable increase in sportswear and less in dresses. Sportswear was on fire, and we kept breaking down classification into departments and funding accordingly. Additional buyers were hired. Management was most supportive. There was never a better time to be a sportswear merchant.

Emily, I was so lucky to have you nearby. Our Saturday trips were so enjoyable because we shared so many overlapping interests.

Love,

Lauren

Chapter Two

Our New Owners—C.H.H.

Dear Emily,

Our new owners showed signs of affluence such as an educational center in California, a highly developed control systems, expensive New York offices, and unnecessary travel.

Thalhimers stores were opened in Lynchburg and Roanoke, Virginia, one large and one smaller store in Charleston, South Carolina, one at Virginia Beach, and finally, Memphis, Tennessee. Negotiations were proceeding in Charlotte, North Carolina, where the prime real estate in Southpark Shopping Center was controlled by the Ivey and Belk families who had not been open to competition. Our white knight had also proved to be our Santa Claus.

Our inventory control systems were years ahead of many of our peer stores. All buyers and divisional were flown to our C.H.H. education center in Anaheim, California for computer training and to view our huge IBM installation. These ego trips were extended to include all store managers, who could have cared less. A few C.H.H. trainers could have flown to Richmond, others to a location in central North Carolina and held schools that would have accomplished more and been more economical. Tickets purchased for $500 round-trip were known to have been exchanged for $2,000 tickets due to last minute rescheduling.

C.H.H. was on a high. They added the prestigious Wanamaker (although slightly tarnished) to their collection of stores. Impressed by their power, they acquired two floors in an expensive location on 37th Street between Broadway and 6th Avenue where we spent valuable market time in poorly planned and executed meetings. A.M.C. meetings were much more informative but sometimes had to be omitted. Soon we were being pressured to buy what the West Coast stores sold, not what our customers wanted, which was our strength. After several locked-horn meetings, management decided to move them to a fine resort near Paling, New York, where we would have fewer distractions. We were strongly encouraged to increase the percentage of our imports.

After several trips to L.A., the Thalhimers merchants sensed a problem. The C.H.H. stores were bottom-of-the-barrel in assortments, outdated merchandise and merchandise presentation. They stood for nothing. The California market belonged to Robinson, Nordstrom, and Macy's. Neiman-Marcus had recognized its mistakes and had found another purchaser. To protect his pride, Philip Hawley, C.H.H. CEO, announced that the company would make greater strides without top-producer Neiman-Marcus. This translated into more pressure on number two—Thalhimers. As profits in California continued to erode, more pressure was put on Thalhimers to conform to the California image. Forbid! Phil Hawley insisted that if we embraced the same resources, profit benefits would follow. With purchases heavily weighted with imports, which carried higher markups, total gross margin would improve. Not being a seasoned merchant, he was counting profits by mark-on, never taking into consideration the sell-through. Poor decisions were made.

Love,

Laurie

Chapter Three

Shopping In Hong Kong

 Dear Emily,

There wasn't any sightseeing here, but enough shopping to occupy any spare time.

The buyers and I made annual January trips to Hong Kong to the A.M.C. Sportswear Fair. Samples had been gathered from all viable resources in the Far East for this well-supported event. The Chinese New Year determined our timing as all orders had to be in the manufacturers' hands before the month-long holiday if we wanted timely delivery.

The Peninsula Hotel and that area resembled New York City. There were numerous 7th Avenue businessmen looking for production, Adkins stores were working with agents, specialty stores had commissionaires. As in a gold rush, no one wanted to be left out.

Due to its popularity, the meeting was relocated from the Peninsula to the Sheridan directly across the street. The ballroom was twice the size of the former. A. M .C. representatives from New York and the Hong Kong office had assembled samples from all the Far East offices. After editing, all samples were sketched with pertinent information and order pads supplied to

157

all buyers. Managers of the satellite offices were on hand to assist. In ten days, enormous orders were written and left.

Every year Hong Kong changed its character; new lavish hotels, more English spoken, more Western dress seen, more Mercedes, more affluence in a small area, but still only bamboo was used for scaffolding.

Unlike Europe, there was little to explore in Hong Kong. You need to visit the Peak only once. The man who introduced Tiger Balm became Hong Kong's benefactor and left the Peak as his memorial. Due to the rocky terrain, the private homes could be counted; the population lived in high-rise apartments. It was not unusual to find apartment buildings in the territories accommodating 5,000. Schools and grocery stores occupied ground floors.

A trip past Happy Valley, the racetracks, took us to Repulse Bay for Sunday buffet on the Verandah. It was superb. We always overate. A bus trip into the new territories gave us a glance of how mainland China must have looked. We saw thousands of boat people huddled into cardboard and scrap lean-tos waiting for their opportunity for another life.

Shopping proved to be Hong Kong's main attraction in the seventies and eighties. It reminded me of Italy in the sixties. The two Chinese arts and crafts stores were filled with hand-embroidered linen sheets and pillowcases, all sizes of hand-embroidered luscious tablecloths, placemats and napkins that retailed for many times more back home. The arts and craft store on Nathan Road emphasized jewelry and jade collectibles, also casual home furnishings. Pure silk lingerie was a steal except sizing was not comparable to ours.

A large building adjacent to the Star Ferry had

hundreds of specialty shops where one could find everything. The water depth by this building was unbelievable. One afternoon I saw passengers of a Viking luxury liner boarding from a gangplank. We enjoyed exchanging conversation with the passengers in a situation I had never expected to witness.

Across the bay on Hollywood Street was an interesting antique market consisting of twenty-five to thirty merchants. In the seventies, old blue Canton ware was available at moderate prices. A few old lacquered screens were seen. We always shopped Ms. Horseman's antique shop at the Peninsula Hotel to find what was collectible and at what price before our shopping trips.

One Sunday morning on Hollywood Street, we witnessed the station of Chinese women. Two women with pails attached to wooden poles resting on their shoulders were moving a large pile of dirt from where it had been dug to a site about a block away. Four men engaged in a board game were directing the move. Unaware of their customs, I adjusted my camera to get a shot of an infant in a basket nearby. The mother dropped her burden and ran screaming toward me. No! No! Later I learned it is bad luck to photograph an infant and the mother would go to any extent to prevent it. An apology was offered as we moved on. Several hours later, we came by the same location to see that all the dirt had been moved; the game was still continuing.

Not everyone enjoyed the native restaurants. In addition to Gaddy's, there were several less formal restaurants in the Peninsula. Occasionally, we would enjoy Peking duck, a specialty at the Mandarin Hotel. Sea-Land would take us out for a meal and view of the harbors from their boat.

The Reynolds Tobacco subsidiary, Sea-Land, made

a decision to invest in larger carriers when the price of oil escalated. That hastened its demise. Larger vessels required more fuel and more days at sea. Added days and West Coast longshoremen strikes contributed to making Sea-Land no longer competitive.

The Stanley Flea market offered a wide variety of sweaters, jackets, blouses, and was a never-miss for some of the buyers. I preferred the Calvin Klein, and Anne Kline locations that sold their better separates at one fourth to one fifth what they retailed for at home. The offerings at the Jade Market varied on visits. For $25 total, an optometrist would duplicate our current glasses while we waited, including stylish frames.

I most miss the great haircuts in Hong Kong. I have had haircuts in New York and many places in Europe but nothing compares to the haircuts in the Sheridan Hotel on the waterfront in Hong Kong. On my second trip, I was told by another merchant that this was by far the best salon. After my first experience, I always had a Saturday morning appointment where in less than one hour I had a haircut, shampoo, blow-dry and pedicure unparalleled. As soon as I was seated in the operator's chair, my feet were placed in a foot tub where they soaked until time for the blow-dry and pedicure. They didn't give manicures. The haircut was always perfect. I received all this pampering for $6 including tip.

When the young man finished my first transformation, I asked him why I couldn't get a comparable haircut at home. His answer: "Your operator studies six to twelve months and learns to cut, color and perm. Here we spend five years learning to only cut hair." His native customers all had straight, thick, black hair. He enjoyed cutting my thick, straight hair; curled and permed hair were difficult for him. Often I have been tempted to go back for a Chinese

haircut and a week of pampering by the Peninsula.
Emily, you would have loved the haircuts here!

Love,

Laurie

Chapter Four

Exploring Virginia

 Dear Emily,

I enjoyed all of our trips exploring Virginia, but Garden Week was my spring special event each year.

Life in Richmond was busy, stimulating and happy, although I arrived with some trepidation. The fact that I had known many of the Richmond Thalhimers' executives for years and had two former North Carolina friends in town made the transition easier. With a full schedule, there was no time for regrets.

Many of my neighbors welcomed me to my new home. I joined a garden club that met at night and set aside one Saturday morning for community projects. There was a jogging track and tennis courts in the neighborhood. Nearby were located a good grocery store, banks, hardware store, restaurants and the finest new high school.

Richmond was well located for me to be able to take advantage of the many historical sites of Virginia. An hour away, off highway 64W was Charlottesville, Jefferson's showcase for his beloved Monticello and also the University of Virginia.

The Charlottesville area was a must for Garden Week visits. The nearby garden of Morven is considered one of the 100 finest gardens in America. The property was developed by a horsewoman from Long Island who was seeking a longer riding season. A plateau, surrounded on all sides by distant mountain peaks, offered a vista seldom rivaled. It was later acquired by Mr. Kluge, a media giant. The walled formal garden was well planned and well maintained. Additional Henry Moore sculptures were added by the new owner, trees lined a drive. The property has been given to the University of Virginia to assure its continuity.

On your way to Monticello, you will see Mackie Tavern, built by Patrick Henry's father and frequented by Jefferson and his friends. Nearby is the home of James Monroe, Ash Lawn, which was designed by Thomas Jefferson. A few minutes away is the restored Montpelier, the home of John Madison—all past presidents of our young country.

Another fun trip was when we headed north on the old 195 to Fredericksburg and visited Kenmore. This outstanding house was home to Colonel Fielding Lewis and Betty Washington Lewis. A drive through the historic district brought us to the Rising Sun Tavern. East to Wakefield, we visited the refurbished childhood home of George Washington.

My favorite destination was further down the Northern Neck to Stratford Hall. The house, built in 1720, may have been home to more patriots than any in our country. Thomas Lee, great-great uncle of Robert E. Lee, planned and built the extraordinary house. He built a massive English manor house rather than a Southern mansion. A Tudor H, it had two clusters of four chimneys on either end, which provided space between the chimneys for the ladies to sea watch for their returning husbands. The Robert E. Lee Memorial

Association Inc. was responsible for restoring the deteriorating masterpiece. The Association opened it to the public in 1936.

The furnishings are superb. Most pieces are American interspersed with a few prime English pieces. Fine English china and luxurious fabrics had to be imported. The Great Hall is the largest paneled room in Virginia. The dining room is recognized as one of the finest rooms in America. Stratford has been a working farm for more than 250 years and now consists of 1508 acres of grazing pasture, woodland and cropland. Don't miss a Southern lunch served in a cabin on the grounds.

We visited Williamsburg until we no longer felt like tourists. Sunday lunch at one of the gourmet restaurants was not unusual. In December, the main attraction is the outstanding judged Christmas door decorations. A visit to the Abbey Rockefeller Museum with its antique toy collection and unusual Christmas tree decorations was on our annual list, as was a magnificent lunch or dinner at the Colonial Williamsburg Inn.

Jamestown and Yorktown were naturals for all history buffs. I admit I spent more time exploring the James River Plantations, which offered a rare peek into early American culture (if you were a large landowner). Virginia fathers adopted the inheritance laws from England. That meant all the land went to the oldest son. This custom accounts for the large tracts of land remaining in Virginia as opposed to the many small farms in adjoining North Carolina. The heavy German population in the border state chose to have their farms divided equally among all heirs.

Accustomed to the beautiful, scenic, less-densely developed beaches in North and South Carolina, Virginia Beach held little appeal. The backup at the tunnel could make a weekend trip a nightmare.

If any state has a Garden Week comparable to that in Virginia, I am not aware. The "week" includes two weekends plus the week when garden clubs all over the state open and exhibit their best gardens. No state has as many original, restored, and reconstructed eighteenth century buildings; many have restored Colonial gardens also. One weekend we would allocate to Richmond, where often several handsome Lawrence Bottomley houses on Monument Avenue would be open. Virginia House with its beautiful gardens and mile-long view to the James River was not to be missed.

The second weekend could take us as far west as Abington or as far east as the Eastern Shore, the Northern Neck and anywhere in between. Anyone interested in architecture, gardens and nature would find nothing more beautiful and stimulating this side of England.

With Washington only two hours north, we tried not to miss any of the major shows at the Smithsonian. The Rodin show in the 1980s included the seldom-traveled "Gates" and drew record crowds. The El Greco show was great and reminded me of my visits to Toledo, El Greco's quaint hometown and his many paintings there and at the Prado in Madrid. My favorite show was the "British Country Houses". This must have been a difficult and expensive show to stage with all the massive furniture and correct accessories. The hand-carved, massive, four-poster beds were dressed with elegant silk and hand-embroidered linens that were hundreds of years old. Needless to add, they were the trappings of royalty. For several hours, one was transplanted to fine castles in England.

There were chartered buses from Richmond to performances at Kennedy Center. Occasionally, we would drive up on Saturdays for lunch and visit the galleries and antique shops. One Saturday, we visited the gardens in Arlington, Gunston Hall, Mount Vernon and the Curtis house.

The Virginia Museum of Fine Art in Richmond was a special treat, and I tried not to miss any of the grand shows they staged. The ambiance of the magnificent building surpasses the severe feeling of our North Carolina Museum. While our board of directors squabbled for years over a location, the cost of construction escalated and the patrons were the people to suffer. The Virginia Museum has been the fortunate benefactor of the Mellon and Lewis Collections. The Lewis family, founder of Best Company, with the help of a capable agent, supposedly assembled the finest Art Nouveau Collection in existence.

For years, the Virginia Museum has staged biannually a themed "Art and Flower Show". The garden clubs of the state are allowed to select a painting from the permanent collection and interpret it through a flower arrangement, which in turn is judged. Afterward, a world-recognized flower arranger will be guest speaker. High Tea and a formal dinner make the show special.

Richmond abounds with interesting houses. To mention a few: the home of Chief Justice John Marshall and Wilton, which is the headquarters of the National Society of the Colonial Dames of America. Richmond, Virginia and Salisbury, North Carolina, are the only two cities I know where Colonial Dames outnumber DAR's. Agecroft is a fifteenth century English manor house moved from England to Richmond in 1858.

St. John's Church in the Church Hill neighborhood is remembered for Patrick Henry's "Liberty or Death" speech. The Poe house is in the same general area. St

Paul's Episcopal Church has beautiful stained-glass windows by Tiffany and is closely associated with the Confederacy. The Virginia State Capitol, designed by Jefferson, was completed in 1788. Hollywood Cemetery is the burial place of two presidents, James Monroe and John Tyler.

Lawrence Bottomley interpreted his eighteenth century architecture as "James River Georgian" and created a high standard for Richmond houses and nearby county estates. His work can be easily observed on Monument Avenue and three larger estates in Windsor Farms. Milburne is my favorite.

Since I lived fifteen minutes from downtown Richmond, I decided I should join a neighborhood church. Several months were spent visiting Presbyterian churches in a five-mile radius of my house. Emily, you kept asking me to include Second Presbyterian downtown to my list. I scrapped the distance excuse, visited Second Presbyterian and liked what I experienced. Dr. Al Winn, the minister, was excellent and, as I was leaving the church after my third visit, he reminded me that after three consecutive visits, one became a member. I gave him the name of my Winston-Salem church, and all was taken care of. The associate minister was always a student from across town at the Presbyterian Seminary. The organist and choir were excellent.

It was a small but active congregation. Although there was no paid cook on staff, women of the church prepared and served lunch to about seventy street people each Monday. Several times a year these same ladies served a lovely hot lunch to the entire congregation, linen tablecloths, napkins and handsome flower arrangements included. The man in charge of altar flowers and all special occasions worked for the

Virginia Park Service and was extremely creative in his arrangements.

Reverend Benjamin Sparks followed Dr. Al Winn as minister. Both were outstanding. Dr. Charles Cornwell, a former Davidson College English professor, enrolled in the Seminary when he was about forty years old. His prayers and sermons at Second Presbyterian reflected his former profession. Although he is no longer married to the well-known mystery writer, Patricia Cornwell, I am told that he has edited each book she has published.

Second Presbyterian was organized and built prior to the Civil War. The handsome stained-glass windows were removed and stored during the war. Afterwards, they were returned to the church that had not been harmed. One window was missing. More than 120 years later, the window was found and dedicated with much pomp and ceremony. The granddaughters of the first minister, Dr. Moses Hoge, were revered members of our congregation.

There was always a strong feeling of Richmond's heavy involvement in the war. It was as if World War II never happened. Except for the fact that Richmonders set fire to their city rather than have their iron works used to the advantage of the Union army, they would boast as many eighteenth century fine homes as Charleston, South Carolina. They do have the numerous fine plantations, but Richmond itself, is today a Victorian city, which is sad.

Emily, they say Richmond is for lovers, but I say it's for history buffs and gardeners!

Love,

Laura

Chapter Five

Time Out

 Dear Emily,

I was as surprised as you were. The first Friday of August 1984, was hot and humid as expected in Richmond. The college student who had hit tennis balls with me had attended summer school in Los Angeles, and we had a 6 p.m. appointment. After twenty minutes of hitting the ball, I had a tight feeling in my chest and took a few minutes break to have some water while the pain went away. After hitting for twenty more minutes, I said that I was tired and hot and thought we should stop.

When I reached my house, I was wet with perspiration. Immediately, I filled a glass with crushed ice and water and sat in the shade on my back stoop. With not a dry thread on me, I went upstairs and slipped into some dry clothes—no bath. By this time, I had pain in my left shoulder and felt nauseated. I was very weak but managed to get to my bed and called nine-one-one.

The life support group was stationed less than five minutes away, and the driver called as he left the station to ask if my door was open. I was upstairs, and both outside doors had dead bolts. The driver calmly replied, "Then, we will have to break the door down." I was sick, but that made me worse. I hung up, crawled to the top of the stairs, and then slid down them, one stair at a time. When I reached the landing, I managed to reach the key and turn it before collapsing on the Oriental throw rug. I couldn't think of going to the hospital with my house unprotected.

In no time, the rescue squad had me on a stretcher and down my front steps. When I looked up, I saw two ambulances with red lights flashing. My lawn was filled with neighbors from the two adjacent blocks. After thanking the rescue squad, I asked why there had been two ambulances dispatched. The driver explained that two vehicles were on location and they made the decision to send both just in case they were needed. Both accompanied me to the hospital.

Fortunately, Hanover County Doctors Hospital was only a few minutes away where I was admitted to the Emergency Room and given a work-up by the doctors on duty. A few minutes later, Dr. Robert Mitchell introduced himself. He was an outstanding, compassionate internist with a residency in cardiology. How fortunate for me. Tests showed that I had an artery with sixty percent closure and another with forty percent blockage. Since I had a stressful job, which required much travel, I was advised to have open-heart surgery. My first hospital stay, unlike today, was almost two weeks. My sister came up from Southern Pines the next day. She and her husband drove up the next weekend. My brother-in-law mentioned that the facility looked more like a four-star hotel than a hospital. I enjoyed the pampering; the furnishings, food and nursing care were outstanding. The nurses looked in often to check on me and to view my ever-expanding flower arrangements that arrived daily.

My brother came up from North Carolina the

second weekend. We had a good visit. My neighbors looked in on him and made him feel comfortable in his new surroundings.

The September market trip was on schedule, and I felt as if nothing had happened. Holiday season surpassed plans. While I was debating if I should have surgery, my cardiologist insisted that if I were his mother, he would insist she have the operation.

Then the decision moved to who would perform the operation. I knew only one person who had undergone the relatively new and frightening operation. Mr. Charles Thalhimer suggested I could go to Dallas, Texas, where Dr. Michael DeBakey had earned fame. A cardiac surgeon at Duke was recommended. Dr. Richard R. Lower, an outstanding and world-renowned surgeon at the Medical College of Virginia in Richmond, was my choice. Dr. Christian Bernard from South African fame had trained under Dr. Lower.

My choice was a good one. The long operation was in mid-February. My lifestyle was not compromised, and for fifteen years, I enjoyed an active life, volunteering, gardening, traveling, playing tennis, jogging and walking. Years later, when I visited my cardiologist for a semi-annual check-up, I was told that the two replaced arteries had closed down, but that two new, stronger ones had replaced them.

After two weeks at home, I started receiving stacks of bookwork from my office: reports to be analyzed, reports to be written, hours of follow-up. At my two-week check-up, Dr. Mitchell told me that I was not ready for hours of concentrated work. He advised me to call a friend and arrange to spend a month in Florida. Taking his prudent advice, a friend and I rented a condo at Long Boat Key on the west coast of Florida. I walked on the beach and lazed around while my friend enjoyed good tennis with people she met.

When I returned to work, my doctor asked me to have my lunch and go to work at 1 p.m. to avoid getting too tired. Had I gone to the office at 9 a.m., I would never have left at 1 p.m. By the second week, I was on a normal schedule.

Thanks to the support of my great staff, our first six months were on plan. The prestigious President's Cup was given to me that year. Following New York and Hong Kong in January, operation and recovery in February and March, by the end of April, life was back to normal in time for fall openings in New York.

My compassion was with the buyers, but I felt it was time to move on to early retirement. With that in mind, I asked for a week extension to my Hong Kong January trip in 1986. A Charlotte friend joined me for the entire trip after our New York office obtained visas and put together an escorted tour of accessible cities. This was ten years after my first trip to Hong Kong, Taiwan, and Korea and another six to eight years before China was prepared for welcoming tourists.

We were allowed to take the train alone to Guangdong (formerly known as Canton). On the two-hour train ride, we saw only one tiny farm truck and several communes where rice farmers lived and labored.

In our train car, we met several retired teachers from the United States and England who were contracted to teach either college English, math, or science for a year in return for transportation, room and board. We were met by a guide who stayed with us for two days and put us on our next flight.

Our hotel was a compromise; accommodations and food were lean. We saw a Peninsula Hotel under construction. Could they offer the same service they were known for in Hong Kong?

The influence of the British colony was evident here in Guangdong and not seen anywhere else on our trip. English was heard often. Products moved between Hong Kong and this city. A year or two later, a four-lane highway connected the seventy-five miles between the two cities, bringing heavy growth to Guangdong.

From Guangdong we flew to Xian, where nearby archaeologists had uncovered 7500 life-sized clay soldiers buried twenty centuries ago to guard the graves of China's first emperors. Buried also were 500 full-sized horses with bronze bits. Xian's bell tower was impressive by night and dated to the Lang time when it was China's capitol and a great trading city.

One day we had lunch where we encountered a large group of Tibetan herdsmen. Both genders were dressed in lightweight leather and smelled terrible. The next day we had lunch at a little rural village where we were served baked sweet potatoes cut into chunks and glazed with crystallized sugar, then rolled in roasted peanuts. Our vegetable was wild asparagus. Pieces of the chicken I didn't recognize and didn't eat. I am telling you this to show that they were not ready for visitors. My friends, the Christians from New York, had gone on an experimental trip the year before and told of finding a large rat in the commode. Our sheets were so dingy we asked for fresh linens, which looked no better than the dingy ones we had. We decided to sleep in our robes.

We encountered tourists for the first time when we arrived in the sprawling city of Beijing. Cranes and sand dust greeted us. I am told that is the same environment twenty-two years later. The Great Wall Hotel had recently opened, but we weren't able to stay there. We did have reservations for dinner there, which was a welcome treat.

Although Chairman Mau died in December 1976, his preserved body was on display in Tiananmen Square ten years later with wide lines wrapped around the square. Today, thirty-two years after his death, his body is viewed in the "Mausoleum."

We finally felt like tourists when our guide took us on the bus out to the Great Wall. Souvenir stands and camel rides told us commercialism had arrived. We were not allowed any currency, so our guide paid for anything we purchased. After Hong Kong, shopping in Peking was not a priority. We did buy a few cashmere sweaters at our hotel.

The Forbidden City was one of the most interesting sites. I kept asking to see a museum. Finally, we were taken to a small museum that held a few scrolls and some pottery. We visited all the tourist sites, but few gardens were in evidence. The contrast between what was televised at the 2008 Olympics and what we found in 1986 is difficult to believe. The spectacular buildings and the many trees we saw added for the games changed the entire setting.

Transportation in Beijing was almost totally bicycles. Some had three wheels and had a small cart attached that might carry a tiny refrigerator (our dormitory size), or a small screen T. V.

We wanted to give our helpful guide a gift, but she refused. She knew she would be searched when she returned to her office. If anything was found, she would be dismissed. Her family, including her grandparents, depended on her income.

After witnessing the constant progress in Hong Kong, I had expected to find further progress in China. Only after Beijing was selected as the site for the 2008 Olympics did China take giant steps to make a spectacular show of modernization to the rest of the world.

Emily, although I am glad I experienced China, it is not on my list of "return visits."

Love,

Laurie

Chapter Six

Signs of Unraveling

 Dear Emily,

What is too good to be true often is. Six busy years flew by. We had opened a new, larger store in Charleston, South Carolina, Roanoke in Western Virginia, Lynchburg, Virginia Beach, and Memphis, Tennessee. Volume had more than doubled under new ownership. Everything seemed good until we reached the bottom line with the parent company report.

Mr. Carter and Mr. Hawley had successfully "put together" a group of stores encompassing the west coast of California: Weinstock's in Sacramento, the Emporium chain in San Francisco, and the Broadway chain in Los Angeles, Southern California and Arizona.

Mr. Philip Hawley joined the Broadway in 1958 as a sportswear buyer (as the classification was poised to explode) and readily became the protégé of Ed Carter. In 1977, Mr. Hawley succeeded Mr. Carter as chief executive and wasted no time in rearranging the finances. He sold a twenty percent share in Harrod's (an ego trip) and went on a buying spree without the needed background or knowledge. In retrospect, he should have observed the changing demographics of California and attempted to adjust the stores stocks accordingly. Instead, he continued to cater to the same conservative moderate-income customer, while Nordstrom's, Neiman-Marcus, and Macy's "ate his lunch". *Wall Street* said, "God gave Carter Hawley Hale Southern California and they blew it." Instead, he invested in various businesses from west to east and as far north as Canada. It was evident that a long-range plan was missing.

Phil Hawley sold Bergdolf Goodman and Walden Bookstores, also a fine specialty store in Montreal, businesses he never should have bought. Each time, he stated that the cash would be used to pay down the debt. Instead, the money was used for immediate operating expenses.

Thalhimers executives began to get pressure from the West Coast. Stuart Kasen became the first non-family president of Thalhimers. Our profits were good but not enough to make up for the heavy inventories, heavy markdowns and high shortages in the Broadway stores. Thalhimers had several divisionals without the proper experience or knowledge to make the best decisions. There were too many meetings and too many changes of strategy. Rather than planning our businesses and executing our plans, we were changing our markdown projections and advertising accordingly—often several times a week. Nothing in my experience had prepared me for firefighting!

Mr. Charles Thalhimer and his two sons left the store. No doubt, they disapproved of what was happening. Mr. William Thalhimer Jr., CEO and older son was on the C.H.H. board and had to have knowledge of what was happening but continued pushing the sale of stock to the employees for their 401K's.

177

Phil Hawley had boasted that C.H.H. was the first store group to be owned by its employees. Their employees were encouraged to invest up to twelve percent of their earnings in C.H.H. stock, which was held in a 401K. Hawley claimed it was voluntary, but many employees said they were coerced. Stock could not be sold as long as one worked for the company.

In the mid-eighties, Phil Hawley decided that C.H.H. stores should have a lobbyist in Washington to force lower import duties on the textile classification. He stopped by Richmond after several Washington trips to convince management to contribute to the costs of a lobbyist. On his first visit, he picked up a sizable amount of money, but interest rapidly declined when we learned his wife was on the payroll. He regaled us by name-dropping all the celebrities he and his wife had met at the Georgetown cocktail parties.

In 1986, Leslie Wexner made a second unfriendly take-over bid for the sleeping monster, offering up to $60 for stock this time. The Golden Parachute Clause was written in after the first offer. Fighting the expensive take-over battle was too much for C.H.H. One can only wonder what if Wexner had won. He has maintained a good batting average with his collection of stores.

Emily, so much was happening at the same time!

Earlier, in June of 1985, C.H.H. held its sportswear meeting at an expensive resort near Purchase, New York. It was up the road from the Pepsi-Cola headquarters located amid acres of lawn, gardens and handsome sculptures. The location was remote but pleasant, the pressure heavy. The buyers and I reviewed the offerings and tentatively sketched out orders at cost/retail. The following day, all stores met to agree on styles and quantities. By this time, only Thalhimers and

Wanamaker represented the East Coast. The bigger volume came from the West Coast stores. They carried the larger stick. We spent the time dissecting, discussing, compromising—some give, some take. The West Coast stores preferred $19.99 see-through blouses. The East Coast customers preferred beautifully tailored shirts or lace-trimmed linens at $30 to $150. C.H.H. insisted that fifteen percent of our open-to-buy be allocated for C.H.H. branded merchandise. Our better customers preferred branded New York merchandise. The commitments we made in Hong Kong each January were far superior to the programs presented by C.H.H.

We left the meeting drained. We had committed to programs we didn't prefer and bought heavier than we wished in order to meet commitment requirements. In the end, we were not allowed to buy what our customers wanted, and what we knew we could sell. The buyers and I were held responsible for the bottom line although many of our decisions were overruled. We were not accustomed to this. What happened to autonomy?

I had enjoyed only good times in my retail career. Living in New York for about two years gave me the confidence to explore the new world for Juniors back in Charlotte. When Mr. Ivey became greedy, I moved to Thalhimers and helped to grow one store to fourteen stores—from $1 million in sales to more than $60 million. Department stores were expanding at a break-neck speed. Meanwhile, I had been named the first female officer for Thalhimers. It was a matter of timing; I was also the first female officer of our A.M.C. group. Ten to fifteen years later, women probably accounted for at least twenty per cent of department store officers.

Aside from the burning passion for the fashion

business, I was motivated by respect for the people I worked with and worked for. I was dedicated to trying to do a good job—always. I never wanted to be the biggest—I wanted to be the best.

Then, when Philip Hawley announced in the semi-annual report that Niemen Marcus' departure would have a positive effect on C.H.H., I lost my respect for the leader of our stores. How could losing the top money producer be positive? He was trying to save face with his peers.

From then going forward, autonomy was forgotten. All ideas and suggestions came from the top down. No suggestions moved from the bottom up. During my career many good ideas had come from the salespeople—the person-to-person conversations on the floor.

When Charles Thalhimer left the company, so did much of the civility. There was a manager who insisted that buyers purchase from his friends when it was not the best choice. Unqualified friends were promoted and protected. Many unprofessional actions had weakened the store morale.

When I was asked to plan the division sales of a new beach store exactly like a mountain store, I knew it had to be a mistake. Our success had always been closely related to the demographic study of each store. During the following week's business trip to New York, I tweaked the sales to produce the total requested. The departments that sold heavy woolens were decreased and the swimwear and active sportswear departments were expanded, but I couldn't endorse the requested plan department by department. In fact, I felt the total sales were over-estimated, but complied. I alone would be held responsible for producing their inflated figures—not the person behind the request.

Emily, it was a perfect way to set myself up for failure!

As I tried to discuss my strategy, there was an explosion on the other end of the communication. There was no logic. Maybe it was pressure from California, but we merchants were instructed to change our direction every week. Civility was lacking.

For the first time, I was losing my passion for retailing. The vehicle was out of control. Professionally, I had gone further up the ladder than I had anticipated. I was given the opportunity to experience more of the world than I had ever dreamed. Lasting friendships had been made. I derived satisfaction from the fact that I joined a good store and was able to contribute to making it a better store. Timing had served me well throughout my career; my sense of timing told me that it was time to make my exit. I said my goodbyes, accepted a huge Baccarat vase too heavy to lift, and moved on to another life. Happy to have spent my working days in the fine stores, I was sad to experience them slipping away.

The numerous lovely gifts from buyers, present and past, and notes thanking me for my assistance in guiding their successful careers were heartwarming and treasured. The manufacturers wrote letters, sent gifts, and filled my house with flowers and plants. The friends you make along the way make the journey special, don't they, Emily?

Not just traditional department stores and long-respected banks, but many of our trusted institutions have collapsed. We can make many excuses but the ultimate culprit is the lack of character of man—individual, corporate and national greed. The sad commentary is that Wall Street and the bankers, which were rescued from the 2008 upheaval by the taxpayer, seemed to have learned nothing. For in 2009, Citibank proposed fifty percent bonus increases. This is just stupid. Their survival is still in doubt. Many of the rescued banks rushed to impose fee increases and charge card interest rates were increased to astronomical heights—greed.

Emily, what has happened to caring, honesty, credibility, humility, morality, and respect? Government officials say one thing and do another: *'absolutely no earmarks!'* equals more of the same.

What happened to all of the money? Having twelve children at home should have prepared Philip Hawley to manage the budget!

If character is learned by example, we still have a distance to go. "Man is his own undoing."

Love,

Laurie

Chapter Seven

Thalhimers, 1842-1992: A Late Bloomer

 Dear Emily,

Here is another history lesson. You won't like the ending. I didn't.

William Thalhimer, a thirty-one-year-old teacher from Germany, opened a small dry goods store in Richmond in 1842. Traveling with him on the ship that docked in New Orleans were Messrs. Kaufman, Stern, and Rosenstock. Mr. Kaufman had plans to join acquaintances in Pittsburgh. The other three men decided to see some of the new countryside on the way. The ticket master misunderstood their broken English and routed the three to Petersburg, Virginia, instead of Pittsburgh. All four later realized their dreams to become successful businessmen in their adopted country. Mr. Kaufman became a partner in Kaufman Brothers in Pittsburgh. Mr. Stern became a partner in Stern Brothers in New York. Mr. Rosenstock settled in Petersburg, Virginia and founded Southern Department Stores. Mr. Thalhimer selected a one-room site adjacent to the Farmer's Market at Main and Seventeenth Streets in Richmond, which grew into a twenty-five store chain with sales of nearly half a billion dollars. The four merchants kept in touch through a round-robin letter, which chronicled their progress and probably was the forerunner of the buying office that was to surface decades later.

Most of Richmond went up in flames during the War Between the States. Thalhimers was not spared. They rebuilt and moved twice before settling in at East Broad Street, between Sixth and Seventh, where it remained from 1922 until it closed. It had expanded and remained a downtown landmark for seventy years. Miller & Rhoads had opened a small store in the adjacent block as early as 1889. As the two companies prospered, they expanded until each store occupied a complete block facing Broad Street. For years, the two larger stores offered the best shopping experience between Washington and Atlanta. The two stores did not cater to the same customers. Miller & Rhoads aimed for the more affluent customer while Thalhimers appealed to the masses.

Not until the decade of the 1960s did Thalhimers become the leading store in Richmond. In ten years, it added as much volume as the first 128 years had contributed. Several moves by the company impacted the growth. Its move into North Carolina was well timed. At the same time, the company moved away from its emphasis on basement and budget merchandise in the Richmond stores. With a more aggressive approach, Thalhimers began to attract the same customers that had shopped across the street, without giving up its own loyal following.

Thalhimers had moved out in front before Miller & Rhoads agreed to merge with Garfinkel and Brooks

Brothers. After the 1967 merger, the gap between Thalhimers and Miller & Rhoads widened each year. Being aggressive merchants, Thalhimers moved into all the larger North Carolina markets with the exception of Charlotte, where Belk and Ivey's controlled the real estate. Two large, well-located Thalhimers stores were added in Richmond.

Thalhimers in downtown Richmond, VA. Photo courtesy of the Thalhimer family collection.

Over time, the Thalhimer Brothers became dedicated to catering to both middle and affluent customers. Top New York architects were employed and given a free hand. Thalhimers supported their merchants with ample-sized stores and were willing to take a risk, which in turn contributed to exciting, interesting stores.

Thalhimers carved out a niche in the markets they served. Service was a priority. Satisfaction or your money refunded—no questions asked. Management was dedicated to finding what the customer wanted and then going to all lengths to supply it. Special orders and the moving of merchandise were business as usual, unlike the situation in today's culture. The Richmond store offered a large bookstore, a coin shop, optician, pharmacy, travel agency, shoe repair, smoke shop and a delicatessen. These were some of the added service departments not found in many department stores.

When the delicatessen opened on the street floor of the flagship store in Richmond, Virginia in 1947, it was the first of its kind in the South. (This was Mr. Thalhimer Sr.'s idea—very European.) It handled hundreds of take-out lunches daily and catered large receptions. Thalhimers' black and white checkered bakery box sent home many six-layer chocolate cakes, lemon chess pies, lemon coconut cakes, Sally Lun rolls, pecan pies, coconut custard pies, and shadow cakes. Out-of-town shoppers always agreed to meet at Thalhimers Bakery as their last stop. This same delicatessen took orders and prepared hundreds of delectable Smithfield hams at holiday times.

Also ahead of its time was the Soup Bar which opened in 1949. In 1955, the Richmond Room opened for lunch, tea, and dinner and became well-known in the area for its chicken Kiev, Chinese chicken salad, and New England and Manhattan clam chowder. Legendary were such seasonal favorites as shad roe and soft shell crabs. Not to be missed were the light, crisp, mouth-watering popovers and rich spoon bread. Few restaurants today could compete.

When the segregation issue came to Richmond in 1960, Thalhimers was the first to change its policies.

After months of vacillating, Thalhimers made the first move by opening their lunch counter, dining rooms, and restrooms to blacks. They moved on to offer equal opportunities in hiring and promoting blacks. Miller & Rhoads, catering to the more affluent customer, did not have as much at stake and hesitated in making a like decision.

Another first for Thalhimers was their move to recognize women as executives and officers before other stores moved.

Emily, I never expected that my hard work would lead to my being the first woman officer at Thalhimers.

Thalhimers led other Associated Merchandising Corporation stores in this action. Today, women fare well in the retail field, but not so in the 1960s. The brothers were progressive merchants who were dedicated to seeing the company grow profitably through honesty, quality merchandise, and service. Women were given an equal chance with men. Bottom-line performance, not gender, was the deciding factor in job assignments, promotions, and salaries. Thalhimers sought to hire capable people and then encouraged them to be creative and to take risks.

Emily, we were on a roll! In the 1970s, new stores were being built and many more were planned for Virginia and North Carolina. Moving into other states was being considered. The brothers William Jr. and Charles decided that the future of the company could be best served by a friendly merger with a company that offered strong financial backing and the know-how to propel the store into a sure future. Their neighbors, Miller & Rhoads, had merged with the Garfinkel Group in 1967. Atlanta-based Rich's had sold to Federated stores in 1976. Thalhimers had managed to rebuff attempts by Allied, but they felt uneasy about the future. Carter Hawley Hale, a California conglomerate noted for its dramatic growth, was selected to be the new owner in 1978. The price tag was $76 million. Philip Hawley, Chairman of Carter Hawley Hale, promised autonomy. Other than added financial support, little change was evident in the Thalhimers stores for years. This was a wise move. Many customers never realized that the company had been sold.

New stores, plus continued growth in the same stores, moved the volume near the $445 million mark by 1990. It looked like a good marriage. After Neiman-Marcus, Thalhimers was one of the top performers in Carter Hawley Hale. In contrast, Broadway, in Los Angeles known as the acquiring store, always seemed to be plagued with profit deficiencies.

Carter Hawley Hale earnings did not measure up to those in the industry. Limited's Leslie Wexner referred to the company as a "sleeping giant" and moved for an unfriendly takeover, first in 1984 and again in 1986. The expensive fight, poor judgment, and a floundering retail empire that Phil Hawley had lost control of hurled the company into bankruptcy early in 1991. Hawley had sold off his newly acquired empire piece-by-piece—Waldenbooks, Neiman-Marcus, Bergdorf Goodman, Wanamaker's, and finally Thalhimers. The money was not used to pay down debt but for immediate operating expenses. Greed, bad decisions, ego, and lack of expertise played havoc with some of the nation's top department and specialty stores.

Mr. Charles Thalhimer, the younger of the two brothers, was president of the stores from 1973 until 1984 when he retired. He spent his working years in the stores where his interest always centered on its people and the merchandise while his brother concentrated on the financial aspects of the firm. Soon Mr. Charles' two sons, Charles Jr. and Harry, both merchandise managers, resigned. They could not have approved of the about-turn of Carter Hawley Hale. As the West Coast stores made poor showings, more pressure was put on the best performers to do even better.

Following Mr. Charles Thalhimer's departure, Stuart Kasen became the first non-family president of the company in 1984. Under his leadership, the stores enjoyed good growth in a heavily promoted environment. It was his and Philip Hawley's doctrine that enough volume would take care of profits. With the West Coast bearing down, soon unsound decisions were being made. Not long after being named CEO, Kasen left Thalhimers to head the Emporium, another Carter Hawley Hale store that was soon to have Nordstrom's as a neighbor. He was there for only a short time.

Thalhimers' new president, Michael Weinberg, from Weinstocks in California, found neglected markdowns and old stocks. He cleared the decks and was making progress in restoring the luster to the stores when he was faced with a slowdown in merchandise arrival due to a cash flow problem with Carter Hawley Hale. When Mr. Weinberg returned from a market trip, he found he had been replaced by the man who had hastened the closing of Miller & Rhoads earlier. This new president was an ex-Meier & Frank Company executive and immediately added lower-priced, poor quality lines. In retrospect, it seemed he was setting up the stores for the new owners.

The taste level and quality of merchandise offered did not meet the standards previously expected from the founding Thalhimers stores. In November, 1990, May Company acquired all holdings of Carter Hawley Hale for $340 million. This purchase included the tarnished

Thalhimers. The decline was hastened by four Thalhimer presidents in six years.

It was the '*May way or the highway*'. They made no attempts to gear the stores to the desires of the customers. When asked if there would be changes made to adjust to the new market, May Company officials said if the '*May way*' was good enough for the fourteen stores they presently owned, it was good enough for Thalhimers. May Company officials had decided months in advance that the downtown Richmond, Virginia flagship Thalhimers plus several other stores would be closed after the profitable holiday season. Meanwhile, these stores were receiving new fixtures, paint jobs, and updated lighting when the bomb fell. Even the Richmond management had not been told until the day of the public announcement. The executive offices in the downtown store had been lavishly redecorated one month and closed the next. With the downtown closing, more than 1000 Thalhimers employees were immediately let go. Many had never held another job. A cloud hung over Richmond. Miller & Rhoads had declared bankruptcy in 1990 after 105 years. Few department stores had outlived them. Downtown Richmond had moved from being a shopping mecca to being a desert.

May Company immediately reduced and eliminated all the better lines of ready-to-wear, china, and gifts. This included newly arrived Oriental rugs from the Middle East, purchased over several weeks the prior year by Thalhimers buyers. Quick to act, but slow to learn, the May Company was forced to return to many of the resources they had eliminated. Never interested in demographics, they managed to come up with a formula that finally appealed to a wide range of customers seeking moderate price lines. Customer service and housekeeping were not priorities.

Richmond was good to Thalhimers, and in turn, Thalhimers had been good to Richmond. Two dozen organizations have benefited from their corporate generosity. The brother's commitment to the community was constant. They served on numerous boards and headed financial drives.

The Charles Thalhimer family had no connection with the business after 1986. In respect and appreciation for the loyal employees who had made up the store family, Mr. Charles Thalhimer gave $1 million to establish the Charles Thalhimer Family Assistance Program announced January 23, 1992 in Richmond. The fund, administered by the United Way was to provide former employees with up to $3,000 to pay rent, mortgages, utility bills, medical expenses, food, and tuition for job retraining and other special needs. If William Thalhimer Jr., CEO, offered any assistance, it was not known.

The city was shocked, saddened, and angry about the closings in 1992, but everyone turned out for the going-out-of-business sales. The name Thalhimers changed to Hecht's and was merchandised from Baltimore.

Emily, times had changed. The demographics had made downtown operations difficult, but Thalhimers' tragic end was traced to the poor judgment of Philip Hawley, who was so interested in becoming CEO of the largest department store group in America, that he neglected the fine stores he was fortunate to acquire with his line of credit. Neither he nor his team had any experience with the operations of better stores. Yet his first targets were Neiman-Marcus, Thalhimers, Bergdorf Goodman, and Wanamaker's. He allowed autonomy as promised until his Los Angeles stores ran into trouble. Then he applied pressure on the better stores to buy more private label programs to improve paper mark-on. Mark-on meant nothing if the Hollywood glitz didn't sell. His recklessness plummeted the stores to depths from which they could not recover. Many former employees resent how Phil Hawley and the store management pushed the sale of C.H.H. stock when they knew bankruptcy loomed. Many were threatened with job loss if they didn't participate in payroll stock purchases. Those employees lost their life's savings through this scheme. Then they lost their jobs.

At Thalhimers, three different management teams with three different directions in just three years weakened Carter Hawley Hale's best performing store.

May Company dropped many of the former Thalhimers resources, promoted low-end and upper-moderate merchandise, and built a loyal following that lasted from 1992-2006.

May Company was bought by Federated and soon after this acquisition, Federated adopted the well-known name of Macy's as the corporate name for the holdings which now accounted for the largest conglomerate of department stores. Macy's cleaned up and reset the stores to give a more updated look. Soon they were paying attention to demographics and stocking better merchandise. If they fail, there is no one else in the department store field to pick them up.

Only Strawbridge & Clothier of Philadelphia outlived Thalhimers as a full-line family involved, publicly traded department store. It is unlikely the kind of service offered by the family owned department stores will be duplicated. The family commitment to the welfare of the areas they served, and the integrity and support were the badges of another era.

Emily, without Miller & Rhoads and Thalhimers, downtown Richmond became a bad dream.

Love,

Lauren

Thalhimers

Above: The line is to see Mao, ten years after his death.
Tiananmen Square.
Below: The Great Wall of China 1986

Part Five:

Long Happy Retirement

*Above: Fifteenth century housing. There are 100 steps to the top.
Dubrovnik, Yugoslavia
Below: The Grand Hotel. Built as home for Kai-Shek. Taipei, Taiwan
1986*

Chapter One

Reconnecting to the Community

Dear Emily,

I'm finally settled back in my house in Winston-Salem. By mid-year of 1986, and after three tenants, workmen had been busy since January, sanding, repairing, painting and adding a large glass sunroom and attached garage. A landscape architect added a meandering curved border at either side of the back lot and a deep woodland garden in the back. The borders were ready for bulbs and perennials in the fall.

Following Dr. Mitchell's advice, I joined the cardiac rehab program at Wake Forest University. Dr. Henry Miller was a pioneer in organized exercise for his heart patients. Arising at 5:30 a.m., two mornings a week, for a 7 a.m. class was not easy for a night person, but it was gratifying.

Reynolda House Museum offered a lecture series, *American Art Discovery*, for those who were interested in becoming a docent. After fifteen years of browsing the European museums, I felt familiar with the Old Masters, but uncomfortable about my lack of knowledge of American art.

The museum occupied the spacious, former home of Mr. R.J. Reynolds—the tobacco tycoon of the early

1900s. The property was given to Wake Forest University by a granddaughter to assure its role in the future.

Working as an educational docent was rewarding in that I learned and enjoyed sharing my knowledge with visitors of the museum. After I enrolled in my Master's studies at Wake Forest, I assisted in arranging fresh flowers for the house because my schedule didn't allow time for tour groups.

My travel schedule and workload had prevented me from being a joiner or a dedicated volunteer. I moved my church membership back to First Presbyterian Church and joined a church circle for the first time. Being a circle leader was enjoyable. I liked meeting new people and visiting the shut-ins with fresh flowers from my new garden. Another circle member and I volunteered to deliver Meals on Wheels twice a month.

Soon I joined Spade and Trowel, one of the oldest and most dedicated garden clubs in town. The club members included several master gardeners, qualified horticulture judges and some great flower arrangers. Flora Ann Bynum was responsible for organizing The Southern Garden History Society and was a strong force behind it all her life. She lived in one of the Old Salem historical homes and was an advisor for the Old Salem Gardens.

As a member of Mary Symington Book Club, I have met some of Winston-Salem's most influential women. For example, a retired organ teacher at Salem College spends her time composing for worldwide commissions. She composed a sacred piece, delivered and presented the commission to a church in Prague, Czech Republic. Another former Salem College professor of Woman's Studies facilitates our book reviews.

Another club I participated in was the Louise Haywood Service League, which sponsors an annual Valentine party for all of the residents at Salemtowne Retirement Home. All proceeds from club projects benefit Salemtowne.

After First Presbyterian Church targeted a younger group, I chose to join another church just a few blocks west—Centenary United Methodist. This church has approximately 4000 members, always has a strong pastor, an extensive educational program, and as strong a music department as any I have known. Varied levels of Bible study are offered to appeal to day or night preferences. A retired English professor from Davidson College offers a lecture series on a pre-announced fiction writer with definite religious influences. Many Wake Forest professors have held lecture series Sundays before church service. Dr. Efind, a Duke Professor of Religion holds dinner lectures in the spring and fall for a long weekend when he concentrates on one book of the Bible. While many downtown churches are struggling, Centenary is reaching out to more people with Power Lunch each Wednesday noon. In the church, interesting discussion groups may be found on about any subject.

With a lot of wonderful friends and acquaintances, Winston-Salem has been a delightful retirement home. I admit I do occasionally miss the big cities, but not for long. Winston-Salem is known as the "City of the Arts". Four local colleges and universities (with emphasis on The North Carolina School of the Arts) are responsible for a level of performance in opera, symphony, drama and dance that is not common for a town of this size and larger.

The Hanes families have been the prime arts supporters in our city. We would not have attained the status we presently enjoy without the support of the Hanes families. Many people are grateful to the Hanes.

Without the personal involvement and generous benevolence of the Hanes families, Winston-Salem wouldn't be respected as "the City of the Arts" today.

Mr. James Hanes set an example when he gave his handsome home and beautiful lake and wooded property for SECCA (Southeastern Center for Contemporary Art) – a first for the area.

Gordon and Copey Hanes have enriched the enjoyment of the arts in the Winston-Salem area and the state of North Carolina. Their gifts have made music and theater available to the masses. For years, Gordon served on the board of the North Carolina Museum of Art, which has been the recipient of much of his fine art collection. Copey consistently serves on many boards. While serving in the North Carolina State Legislature, Gordon introduced a bill proposing a state supported school for the arts. When presented the next year, it readily passed. Gordon and his friends were able to secure Winston-Salem as the site of the coveted school.

Copey insists that the Moravians and their German heritage are responsible for Winston-Salem's love of music and the arts. Granted, but leaders such as Hanes, Reynolds foundations, Grays, and many others have passed the torch to the next generation. The fourth generation is entrenched.

Few people leave an imprint on the arts as did Philip Hanes, who died in January 2011. The Winston-Salem Arts Council was the first in America and he was sought for advice by many groups. He had a leadership role in the founding of the North Carolina School of the Arts, now part of the State University system–another first. His support and enthusiasm paved the way for the exciting downtown arts and restaurant district, as well as the heavily booked Stevens Center.

While Wachovia Bank and Duke Power were acquiring farms in adjacent Virginia to dam and flood for electric power, Philip Hanes, Wallace Carroll who was the editor of our paper, and others with clout were able to preserve for posterity the world's second-oldest river–the beautiful New River.

Although the Atlantic Coast Conference recently expanded to embrace schools as far north as Boston and as far south as Miami, North Carolina remains the basketball hub. It seems that Duke, Carolina, Wake Forest, or North Carolina State University is usually represented in the finals. Basketball is stronger, but football attracts many followers. Golf and tennis offer great facilities and attract many of the outdoor fans.

Emily, I'm walking three days a week and I hope you're walking as well. For years, I enjoyed tennis every Monday morning and often on Wednesday mornings with another group. I also took advantage of a pool two mornings a week year-round. I highly recommend water therapy.

Love,

Louise

Chapter Two

Retirement Travel Leads to World's Finest Store

Seventh Heaven—Fashion floor at David Jones store. Courtesy of David Jones archive.

 **Dear Emily,**

Stumbling into David Jones in Sydney, Australia was my serendipity. Before I retired, thirty to forty percent of my time was spent traveling and I looked forward to the time I could make my own schedule. After five months spent getting settled, the travel bug returned. Could it be that the more of the world one sees, the more one wants to see?

It didn't take much persuading to convince me that there were links missing in my coverage of the United States. I had seen the vast area from the Mississippi River to the West Coast only from 30,000 feet up.

In September, a friend and I took an extended trip to visit the National Parks beginning in El Paso, Texas and ending in Denver, Colorado. Among the many outstanding highlights were Santa Fe, Mesa Verde, Monument Valley, Zion, the Grand Canyon, Yellowstone, Salt Lake City, the Grand Tetons, Jackson Hole, Crazy Horse and Mount Rushmore. A tour of the Canadian Rockies the following year convinced me that one need not leave America to enjoy some of the world's most beautiful scenery and to stay at some of the world's finest hotels—the Fairmont Group.

My sister, a well-seasoned traveler, planned and executed two outstanding educational trips each year, the proceeds going to a fund for the local historical association. Those I enjoyed most were: Spring Pilgrimage to Natchez, Kentucky Horse Country and Races, Shaker Village, Georgetown, South Carolina rice plantations and hunting estates, Nashville, Tennessee, Franklin, Tennessee and the Hermitage, Winterthure, Longwood Gardens, Chads Ford, New

England Fall Foliage—including Deerfield, Stockbridge, and the new museums of Grandma Moses and of Norman Rockwell.

A friend and I joined the North Carolina Friends for Understanding to visit Nairobi, Kenya for a week spent with the natives learning and enjoying their culture. Since it was migration time, we could not resist adding a week and a most illuminating safari.

We roughed it daily to see the herds of animals close up as they went for water each morning and playfully traveled in the late afternoon as families. Gourmet dinners and comfortable lodgings were scheduled at the grand "watering holes". We lunched at Mt. Kenya Club and visited "Treetops" where young Princess Elizabeth and her husband Prince Phillip were honeymooning when her father died and she became Queen.

One mid-January to mid-February a tennis-playing friend and I took a lovely condo on the extreme west coast of the Algrave, Portugal before the area had been fully developed. Since the Algrave is only about eighty miles long and approximately thirty miles deep due to the encroaching small mountain range, we were able to explore the entire area. We loved having lunch in the quaint villages where a glass of red wine, delicious homemade soup and freshly baked bread were memorable.

Our waterfront condo set on a rock ledge afforded spectacular views. On our way to breakfast in town we would walk through ancient grottos but on our way back we had great expanse of sand.

Our church at the time felt safe in sponsoring an educational tour to Israel and Egypt. This trip was meaningful from the morning we arose to see the sun rising over the Sea of Galilee, to the sites of miracles, sermons, and the place called Gethsemane.

Our hotel in Cairo was new and near the pyramids and the Sphinx but most food was off-limits. We did enjoy the museum and its fabulous King Tut treasures. Sue and I took the overnight train to Luxor to visit the Valley of the Kings and walk among the relics of Biblical times.

The professor at Wake Forest University who taught the class "German Literature from Medieval Days Until World War II," escorted a group of students to Germany each summer that was coordinated with the Institute of European Studies. In 1990, the trip included the "Passion Play" at Oberammergau and ten of our class decided to go.

I left five days early and visited Budapest. The Hungarians were celebrating their recent freedom from forty years of domination by Russia. I was impressed by the happiness and spirit of the people who were so kind to me. The National Museum has the best collection of Spanish Art other than the Prado. I enjoyed this unplanned visit—Elizabeth Island, my delightful hotel, excellent food, sightseeing and my hydroplane trip to Vienna to meet my group.

Our first lecture at the University of Vienna expanded our knowledge of the illustrious history of Austria and its love of the arts. The government is so dedicated to the continuation of the appreciation for the arts that it provides free tickets to every school child each year to take the family to a performance—usually opera. In contrast, it seems the budgets for the arts in the United States public schools are being cut.

Oberammergau was well-orchestrated, from housing and feeding the guests, to staging a grand performance of the Passion Play which was repeated every ten years. I felt that the well-intended production had been commercialized. The small town of 5,000 inhabitants swelled to 15,000. The guests were allowed forty-eight hours to absorb the Passion play, spoken in German, and to enjoy the park-like village. The merchants had spent years getting their stocks ready. I was told by our host that 93% of the German population claimed on their tax forms to be Christians, yet only 0.5% attended a church. Their tax revenue supports the beautiful churches as museums and tourist attractions.

Prague, Czech Republic, and East Germany became interesting destinations one year after the Wall fell. I was not prepared to find the world's finest original Gothic architecture in Prague. Our stay was far too short to enjoy the Old Town, the museums, the local arts and crafts and to hear of the native encounters with first German then Russian domination. There were still many shops of all Russian-made merchandise. Only people over forty-five years of age could recall former days of freedom.

Dresden was showing signs of recovery, but it was sad to see all of the destruction caused by massive bombings. Apartment dwellers living in cinderblock "chicken houses" looked across the street to handsome nineteenth century apartment buildings, reminders of how they once lived. When I asked about the destroyed Dresden Cathedral, I was told that due to the cost, it most likely would not be rebuilt. Many years later, I was delighted to learn that when the new Dresden Cathedral was dedicated, Queen Elizabeth attended. We loved the folk art museum as well as the new opera house.

Leipzig, the home of so many influential musicians, seemed not to have suffered the extent of destruction as Dresden. St. Thomas Church, where Martin Luther lectured and posted some of his edicts was also the meeting place of the dissidents who planned the uprisings that touched off the fall of the Wall in the winter of 1989. History permeated the city.

In 1991, Berlin's recovery was evident everywhere. The stark, new, modern architecture juxtapositioned against all classical buildings created a different-looking city. We visited the Wall Museums, selected a piece of the Wall, and visited Pottstown and Brandenberg Gate near our hotel. It was not a beautiful city.

I couldn't leave the city without visiting one of Europe's largest department stores—KDW. The store was extremely large and included all classifications of merchandise. It reminded me of Macy's 34th Street in the 1940s and the 1950s.

A twenty-four-day tour of the gardens of Italy escorted by a college horticulture professor, started in Venice and ended in Sicily. Nothing was more breathtaking than the view from Sorrento of the azure water interspersed by a curving, rocky shoreline. Many of the fine Italian gardens were classical in design—shaped shrubs, fountains, stonework and grottoes, but when an Italian man selected an English or French wife, her influence was reflected by more colorful plantings.

***

Three of us joined a group for a two-week experience in Australia, and then decided to add ten days for a New Zealand tour. Sydney proved most interesting to me. We were fortunate to obtain symphony tickets to the famous Sydney Opera House, which is probably the most photographed, modern building in the world. The Norwegian architect never saw the completed structure due to a controversy.

On the way to the library to research the department stores in Australia, I accidentally discovered the finest remaining department store in the world. David Jones Limited had been a member of A.M.C. when I joined Thalhimers. I recognized the name, nothing more.

David Jones, born in Ireland, arrived in Sydney in 1836 and opened a general store with emphasis on "the best and most exclusive goods". Today it operates seventeen premium department stores in Australia. It is claimed to be the oldest department store in the world still trading under its original name. It is also the world's finest remaining department store. Harrod's is not in the same league since the Egyptian brothers took over the operation.

David Jones Limited—World's Finest Department Store. Sydney Australia, one of two downtown stores. Photo courtesy of David Jones archive

My heart was racing as I entered the door of the flagship store. The street floor was spacious with wide aisles and large fresh flower arrangements.

To get an overview of the entire store I took the escalator to Seventh Heaven, the Fashion Place. It was laid out as Rue de Riviera with boutiques on the side streets. Six or eight Paris designers each had his space: Lacroix, Armani, Valentino, Ferre, and Versace. Since couture clothes require good accessories, there were shops for Gucci, Vuitton, Ferragamo, and others. All of this, plus huge fresh flower statements and a harpist!

On the sixth floor, I found European sportswear including $500 swimsuits. Everything was imported from Europe, tasteful, beautifully displayed, and the sales people were well trained.

Dizzy from finding something I didn't believe still existed, I found the personnel office and someone with whom to share my feelings. We had a great visit and the personnel manager offered to send me pictures and a biography of the store. I told her I was working on a thesis about the demise of the department store in America.

The next day I returned to the store with a traveling friend. We found a huge button department in a sub floor, another thing we thought was non-existent. The selections and the service were exceptional.

David Jones has weathered and grown strong in Australia where the shift has been from department stores to specialty retailers and suburban malls. Their branding, a black and white houndstooth check pattern, is one of the most-recognized corporate entities in Australia. Family involvement and holding on to their goals for 172 years have contributed to their claim of the finest department store in the world today. They have closed stores and opened them as they concentrate on "low-risk, high-return locations". In my personal observations, I believe they benefit from the proximity and prosperity of Japan. We visited an exclusive Japanese development near the Gold Coast. Casinos depended highly upon Japanese gamblers. My kudos to the finest department store I have ever visited. It was the highlight of my trip—experiencing the world's finest store!

The overwhelming discovery of the David Jones store reinforced my belief that family is the best replacement of the footprint of the founders.

DAVID JONES (AUSTRALIA) PTY. LIMITED

6 November, 1991

Louise Thomas

Winston Salem, N.C.

Dear Louise,

Please accept our apologies in our delay in responding to you letter September 26, 1991. The Archivist has passed your letter on to our department.

I have enclosed colour transparencies of our Elizabeth and Market Street stores as you requested. I do hope that we are not too late in replying.

If there is anything else we can assist you with please don't hesitate to give us a call.

Yours sincerely

Fiona Birdsall
Public Relations Officer

Like most businesses, the department stores that were controlled by the founding family members seemed to contain a vitality and endurance unmatched by those operated by hired outside personnel. John Wanamaker was involved in day-to-day operations until his death at age eighty-four. Mr. Wanamaker's epigram was "The best fertilizer for the farm is the footprint of the farmer". His son, Thomas, who had concentrated primarily in the New York store, died young. The other son, Rodney Lewis, became the sole owner of the two stores. He soon became financially involved in the construction of Wanamaker's "America", a plane commanded by Robert Byrd, and also the first tri-motored crossing to France. He lived only five years after his father's death. His holdings were administered in the interest of his children. The Wanamaker name never again appeared on the list of directors of the store.

Marshall Field's was never the same after the death of the founder and the visionary. He and Harry Graham Selfridge impacted the retail business more than others. When Selfridge was not included as a partner, he left and opened Selfridge of London—still a viable department store.

Personal service is what set Marshall Field's apart. "Nothing is impossible at Field's". "We'll deliver a needle, and we'll pick it up". Over the years, many unusual requests were made and met.

His son died in a tragic accident. His grandsons were successful in the newspaper business; Marshall Field III started the *Chicago Times*, Marshall Field IV became business publisher of the *Sun Times* and chairman of Field Enterprises. Unfortunately, the young men were not interested in retail.

Dick Rich is another example of the end of a

dynasty. Rich's was a household word in the state of Georgia. It was Rich's who saved the cotton farmers in World War II when exports to Europe ended. Bales of cotton were piling up on the streets of small towns when Rich's spearheaded buying the cotton at four cents per pound above the going price, which allowed the farmers to survive. In 1930 when Atlanta couldn't meet the teachers' payroll, Walter Rich advised the mayor to wire script for $645,000. The teachers cashed the script at full value. Rich's waited until the city was able to repay it.

When Dick Rich died in 1975, he was identified with all the major efforts to save Atlanta's central city. He was instrumental in building an $8.1 million arts center, which included the existing High Museum of Art in Atlanta.

Joel Greenburg, son-in-law of Harold Brockey, the CEO of Rich's, became Rich's president and soon started looking for a "white knight" to purchase the stores. Dick Rich's son, Michael, opposed the sale. "We had some stock but not control. A healthy amount of stock was in trust and the bank wanted to sell it."

Rich's was bought by Federated Stores. There was no more Rich family in the store and no more Rich's in Georgia. In the 1970s, Rich's had received sixty cents of every dollar spent in Atlanta on comparable goods. No other A.M.C. store could make a similar claim.

I was fortunate to have had lunch with Mr. Dick Rich and Mr. Charles Thalhimer at the "Artists and Writers" in New York City. Not long afterwards, A.M.C. held a meeting at Rich's, and Mr. Rich invited two of us to his home before our group proceeded to dinner at a downtown club. As late as the 1980s, one could ride the elevator or walk the halls of A.M.C. headquarters at 1440 Broadway and speak to some of the world's great merchants—Mr. Dayton, Mr. Hudson, Mr. Strawbridge or Mr. Thalhimer.

Mr. Stanley Marcus was my dinner partner in Richmond on two occasions when he was promoting one of his newly released books. I shared my pleasant experience visiting his Dallas store, and we had many common interests. He later read my thesis and introduced me to his publisher who suggested rewriting it in first person. I was fortunate to work with his only son the short time Neiman-Marcus was owned by C.H.H.

Mr. Stanley Marcus was dedicated to everything beautiful, quality and tasteful. He recalled how shocked he was each time he returned from Europe to encounter the tasteless, vulgar dress of the people at Kennedy Airport. Who will set the standards for the next generation? Without tastemakers like Dorothy Shaver and Stanley Marcus, who will help raise the bar?

On one of my C.H.H. trips to Los Angeles, I had dinner with Mr. Stanley Marcus' son, Richard, who later served as president of the company. At that time we were sister stores and we had discussed sharing some of their dress programs. I asked him whose idea it was to give points for purchases and awards. He said that the idea came from the president of American Airlines, Robert Crandall, who was the originator of mileage points. I said that I knew Robert Crandall. He was from Winston-Salem and his father had worked for Thalhimers. Richard assured me that the two Robert Crandalls couldn't be the same man. The Dallas resident he knew was from Newport, Rhode Island and not Winston-Salem. I dropped the subject but could only muse that successful men often forget their roots. He is frequently a guest on nightly business news programs. With a thick Southern drawl, I wonder how many people he convinced of his Newport background.

Emily, I marveled that the David Jones store survived when another greedy Aussie came to America to do his damage.

Love,

Laurie

Part Six:

What Really Happened to the Grand Department Stores?

Above: Hong Kong Harbor 1985. Louise and sportswear buyer Martha Moore.
Below: The Charles Bridge overlooking Old Town, Prague. 1991. Louise and her friend Nancy Thomas.

Chapter One

From Peddler to Grand Stores

ear Emily,

It's time for me to answer your question about the disappearance of the fine department stores we experienced in New York City. The great department stores of this nation trace their roots to the country peddlers and the country stores. Peddlers at first walked trails and carried backpacks filled with essentials. As the customers' needs expanded, a wagon was fitted with the basics plus a few frivolous extras: lace, ribbons, shawls and silk. The "Yankee Peddler" flourished for many decades.

Some of this country's successful entrepreneurs started as peddlers: Thomas Edison, Jim Fish and Cyrus McCormick. Experience gained from peddling led to the founding of Macy's, Gimbel's, Rich's and Sak's Fifth Avenue.

As towns sprang up, country stores gave way to dry goods stores and general stores that evolved into some of the first department stores in the United States. The definition of the department store has changed over the years. The name of the first department store has not been confirmed but is generally credited to have been in Paris, France.

A. T. Stewart and Company and Lord & Taylor trace their beginnings to the same year, 1826, in New York City. Not until years later could either be termed a true department store. Both founders were Englishmen and probably were influenced by stores on the continent. At first, the department store was an expansion and refinement of the general store that catered to all people, townspeople and rural inhabitants. Often the founder left his footprint, which lasted several generations,

After World War II and the housing explosion, a department store was expected to have a furniture floor, an appliance floor, silver, china, glassware, table and bed linens, and ladies', men's and children's apparel and shoes. With the arrival of the furniture store, appliance store and carpet stores, the make-up of the department store changed. Outstanding service and quality merchandise were synonymous with the early stores.

The better specialty stores today are Neiman-Marcus, Nordstrom's, Sak's Fifth Avenue, and Bergdorf Goodman. These stores target the customer who expects edited selections of better merchandise and personalized services. With the arrival of the mall and the proliferation of the small specialty shops representing classifications once sold only in department stores, the competition was greater.

For decades, most of the merchandise came from England and consisted of anything not tasteful and not suited for the domestic market. The Machine Age brought mass production, and isolation had not helped the taste level here. The World's Fair introduced in the late 1800s assembled the best of the world's goods and contributed to improving the taste of the Americans. Fairs, followed by museums, were meant to justify the huge amounts of money spent raising the public taste.

The American Museum and the American department store made their appearance at about the same time. By 1900, the department store had arrived in every large city in America: Marshall Field's, the Fair, and Carson Pirie Scott in Chicago; Bloomingdales, Lord & Taylor, B. Altman, Bergdorf Goodman in New York; Wanamaker's and Strawbridge & Clothiers in Philadelphia; Filene's in Boston; Hudson's in Detroit; Rich's in Atlanta; Bullock's and Robinsons in Los Angeles; and I. Magnin in San Francisco.

Before this time, big money had been made in wholesale. Many stores opened wholesale divisions as well as workrooms to accommodate their customers. (Fabrics were the dominate sellers.) After wholesalers exploded, the stores concentrated on retail trade.

The stores, many resembling grand chateaux, were often built around courtyards flooded with light. The spacious floors were perfect galleries, and soon Marshall Field's and Wanamaker's were exhibiting art bought in Europe. At the same time, the museums failed to compete. Displays were poorly hung and lit. There was little provision for comfortable seating and ventilation was poor. Creative merchants recognized their advantage and capitalized on it. The president of the Metropolitan Museum of Art told a group of department store executives that their influence was far greater than all of the museums.

Marshall Field's new store featured a dome by Tiffany, a Louis Quatorze salon for gowns, an Elizabethan Room for fine linens, an Oak Room for antiques, and a French Room for lingerie. In Philadelphia, Wanamaker installed the first electrical elevator in any public building. In his New York store, he included a twenty-two room private home used for model room displays.

The decades following World War II brought a demand for housing as never before seen in America. Department stores were setting aside thirty to forty percent of their space to home furnishings.

In the 1950s, this atmosphere spawned Korvette's, the country's first discounter. Although Korvette's was not around twenty years later, the imprint is still vibrating in the retail world. The Fair Trade Law breakup in 1952 and the world of discount trading today can be traced to Eugene Ferkauf's revolutionary actions.

In the 1930s, the introduction of rayon made a big impact on dress sales. This made a ready-made dress available for special occasions. To a woman accustomed to dressing in wool, cotton or linen, rayon possessed the magic of silk. With the price of cotton and other natural fibers exploding, expect more rayon and synthetics to replace the finer fabrics. These synthetics are not favorable to tailoring and will change fashion forever.

Meanwhile sportswear was gaining popularity. Active sports, running, basketball and tennis were responsible for getting women out of the metal-stayed corsets. Sun worship in the 1930s was responsible for the popularity of skimpy swimsuits. World War II also had lasting effects on the way women dressed and brought the acceptance, reluctantly, for pants to appear other than on the job.

Since the 1960s, the country has had an unflappable love affair with sportswear. Dresses have suffered.

With the affluent customers came the hunger for exciting merchandise from abroad. Whereas the grand old stores had long been dependent on the European continent for better merchandise and ideas, the jet made it practical for many smaller stores to compete. In 1958, Ivey's sent two merchants and the advertising manager to Europe ahead of the pack.

In 1966, Mr. Stanley Marcus was impressed by the promotion of French merchandise in the Nordiska store in Stockholm. The following year, Mr. Marcus introduced the French Fortnight, a two-week extravaganza that brought customers and merchants from all over the world. The following year, Great Britain was featured; the third, Italy.

Every merchant peer tried to emulate the success of Neiman-Marcus and many store buyers were spending time and money in Europe. Fall Fortnight, staged in October, stimulated sales during a slow season between fall and holiday for many department stores. They flourished until one-upmanship became difficult. Rising prices in Europe hastened the demise of the exciting but expensive Fortnight.

The population move to the suburbs after World War II had attracted stores to do likewise. These suburban stores boomed and caused a decline in downtown sales. From the late 1960s through the 1970s and the late 1980s, merchants expanded wildly, although interest rates were also rising. Malls were ever opening, and merchants felt pressured to be included.

Emily, the customer has changed, but so did retailing.

Love,

Laurie

Chapter Two

Four Uninformed, Aspiring Men Play Havoc With the Fine Stores

Dear Emily,

You know greed probably didn't start with Esau and Jacob, but it reached its peak in 2008-09 with the bankers and Wall Street. As early as the late 1970s, four ambitious men began plotting the turbulence in the department stores. They were responsible for change in ownership, the sale and closing of many stores, loss of jobs and the loss of stock and retirement funds for hundreds of thousands of employees. They hastened the end of some of our nation's finest stores. These men were Philip Hawley, Angelo Arena, Bob Campeau, and George Herscu. The first two passed as merchants. The latter two were real estate developers. All were in over their heads.

I became aware of corporate greed as I watched Philip Hawley aim to be the nation's largest retailer and soon. Without the qualifications to run the stores he had been "handed on a silver platter," he raced to acquire stores. Giddy from the vision, he started at the top. Neiman-Marcus was acquired with money from the sale of stock of Harrod's of London. Then one of Canada's finest specialty stores, Holt Renfro was added. Spreading his wings, he bought Walden Bookstore and Contempo Sportswear—not in keeping with the other acquisitions. Again, with taste for the better, he bought Thalhimers, Wanamaker's and Bergdorf Goodman.

Mr. Stanley Marcus became disenchanted and protected the future of Neiman-Marcus by finding another buyer. Today, Neiman-Marcus, Nordstrom's, Saks and Bergdorf Goodman remain the largest fine specialty stores in our country. The survival rate of specialty stores is much higher than that of the department stores. Leslie Wexner, primary owner and CEO of The Limited, recognized C.H.H. as a sleeping giant and made two takeover attempts. To try to stay afloat, Mr. Hawley sold stores while still investing in new stores. His folly overtook him, and bankruptcy was declared in 1991, thirteen years after acquiring Thalhimers. The entire trip was the result of poor judgment, ego, greed and gall.

Andy Areno and Phil Hawley were cut from the same cloth. Their paths often crossed. Luckily, they didn't team up. Areno was a cosmetic buyer at Broadway, Los Angeles. Philip Hawley bought sportswear in the same store. After serving as vice-president in Bullock's in L.A., Areno became vice-president at the Emporium in San Francisco. He moved to become president of Neiman-Marcus under C.H.H. ownership. Here he caught the fever to go national, which he carried with him to Marshall Field's as chief operating officer. Andy was scarcely settled in when the C.E.O., Joseph Burham, died suddenly. This propelled Andy into the position of chief executive officer of Marshall Field's just six weeks after he arrived in Chicago. At the same time, his friend, Philip Hawley made an offer to purchase outstanding shares of Marshall Field's stock at $36 a share. Some say the timing was part of the plan, but Philip Hawley denied this.

Areno hastily launched an ill-directed acquisition program that soon left Marshall Field's no longer a cash-rich store—Frederick Nelson of Washington State, then the Union, in Columbus, Ohio, Halle Brothers in Cleveland and Ivey's in Charlotte, North Carolina. His actions lacked focus, the stores suffered and Field's showed a loss in 1980.

Andy Areno and Phil Hawley adopted the same poor strategies that led to failure. Andy was forced to sell some Chicago property and Halle Brothers was sold. Field's stock price was hovering around $14 per share. Rumor was rampant of a takeover by Carl Ichan and Macy's when Field's was sold to BATUS, a large London conglomerate. The price was $10 less than the offer that had been proposed four years earlier by C.H.H. The total cost to BATUS was $365 million for Marshall Field's and its subdivisions—a steal! Areno had squandered more than $400 million in less than four years and robbed Chicago and the nation of its finest stores.

Then, with the experience of Philip Miller and the backing of BATUS, the future looked bright for Field's. Miller brought his Neiman-Marcus experience and was reputed to be a sound merchant. To restore some of the former luster, $110 million was spent on the flagship store so long neglected. The far-flung stores also needed renovating. Ivey's of Charlotte was a better fit and represented what Marshall Field's originally stood for. The Ivey buyer said that nothing changed except the addition of the famous Marshall Field's mints.

Eight positive years suddenly came to an unexpected end when BATUS observed the retail scene in America and wanted no part of it. Marshall Field's was for sale along with Bonwit Teller, B. Altman, Bloomingdale's, Rich's, Filene's, Foley's and Burdines. Sak's Fifth Avenue and Ivey's were added to the impressive list of unsold stores.

Dayton-Hudson, based in Minneapolis, acquired Field's for $1.04 billion in 1983 and again the flagship store was refurbished to try to restore its former appeal. The Tiffany clocks and the name reigned until Macy's acquired it in 2006. The landmark clocks and the beloved Marshall Field and Company sign were removed.

Until this day, Chicago has not accepted the loss of the grand old emporium. Marshall Field's was famous for the slogan: "Give the lady what she wants." They advertised that they would sell you a needle, deliver it, and pick it up the next day for credit. Marshall Field had only one peer: John Wanamaker. Field was known for his integrity, character, and community philanthropy and leadership. He was the first major benefactor to the Field Museum of Natural History. The Art Institute of Chicago, the John Shedd Aquarium, and the University of Chicago have all benefited from the generosity of Marshall Field.

Thousands of Chicagoans protested; many marched and boycotted. Field's and Chicago were synonymous for 150 years. Field's set the standards for world-class quality in services, fashions, merchandise, food and culture. According to a current blog, *"The world recognized Marshall Field's; Macy's just doesn't make it."*

As a young French Canadian, Robert Campeau gave up his formal education at age fourteen in the eighth grade. From a poor family, he was known as a hard worker and a dreamer. After observing his cousin who had built a house for $1,000 and sold it for $3,200, Bob Campeau saw an opportunity and pursued it.

In the seventies, with a huge ego and the money to support it, Campeau decided to take on Toronto, Canada's largest English-speaking city. His French connections had served him well in his being awarded many federal projects in Ottawa and Hull. After surmounting numerous obstacles, the Toronto Waterfront Development was a success.

He lost money on a tasteless Toronto Hotel, until he sold the $7 million hotel to a Hong Kong investor for $81 million.

By 1986, Campeau Corporation had assets of $1.5 billion and revenue of $200 million. He was aware of the big game being played across the border. General Electric had acquired RCA for $6 billion. Philip Morris spent $5.6 billion for General Foods and Kolberg Kravis Roberts paid $5.4 billion for Beatrice, owner of Krispy Kreme.

After doing his homework, Campeau decided the best route to make up for missing the area of shopping center realty, the mall, was to purchase a large merchandiser in the United States. He decided on the eleventh-largest general merchandiser, Allied Stores. Allied owned twenty-four divisions made up of specialty and department stores. Campeau met his equal with sixty-seven-year-old Thomas Maciore, Chairman and CEO of Allied Stores. Both were poor boys who had worked their way up. Maciore, in contrast to Campeau, had a law degree from Columbia University.

Both men solicited help and Campeau came out the winner. He paid Allied $3.5 billion plus $116.3 million and break-up fees for a total of $4.3 billion. Campeau felt exonerated and First Boston boasted, "This is the dawn of a new era of merchant banking."

The biggest asset that Campeau brought to the deal was his ego. But how would he pay down the debt? First, he got rid of the least-profitable stores. Suddenly, the market was flooded with stores. The security of thousands was shaken. While still digesting the Allied purchase, Campeau advised First Boston that a year had passed since the Allied deal, and he was ready for another target. They settled on a plan to acquire Federated Stores, the fifth-largest retailer and second-largest department store group. Unfortunately, Federated was vulnerable at the time. When the market crashed on October 19, 1987, Federated Stores' stock fell to a low of $29 before selling at around $33. (First Boston had estimated the takeover would cost about $70 a share). To raise money, Campeau agreed to sell his jewel—Brooks Brothers—to Marks and Spencer of London for $770 million. He then made arrangements to sell Federated. Bloomingdales was the shining star. Filene's and Foley's divisions would go to May Company (Foley's had recently merged with fashionable Sanger's). Macy's CEO approached Federated for a merger and Macy's entered the bidding.

Campeau persevered. Macy's Finkelstein agreed to withdraw from the bidding in return for the right to buy I. Magnin and Bullock's for $1.1 billion. Campeau agreed to pay Macy's $60 million to cover expenses. Howard Goldfeder, CEO of Federated, received a $7 million bonus.

It was the largest takeover in history not involving an oil company. Campeau paid more and got less than he had contemplated. Filene's and Foley's went to May Company, I. Magnin and Bullock's went to Macy's. He hastily sold off Federated's Gold Circle, Filene's Basement, Main Street, The Children's Place, and closed five Sterns stores. He played havoc with some good stores.

Campeau didn't help matters when he attended an AIDS benefit staged by Bloomingdales. He had a knack for talking about matters he knew absolutely nothing about—retailing: he dominated the conversation with Marvin Traub, the admired chairman of Bloomingdales.

Shock and turmoil prevailed in the former Federated and Allied stores. Customers complained of lack of service and merchandise. The morale of the stores couldn't have been worse. Campeau made an offering of Federated junk bonds to provide financing, but finally ended paying sixteen and seventeen percent interest. Oblivious to the problem, he announced that he and a partner were going to develop fifty to one hundred malls with a Bloomingdales or Burdines anchoring each. Customers and employees were aware of problems but the public didn't know until an announcement was made at a stockholders meeting on September 12, 1989. Bloomingdales, the crown jewel of Federated, would be sold: properties in Canada were put up as collateral. Campeau was drowning in a $9.5 billion debt. Bloomingdales stock dropped to $13.50. They lost $191 million in six months versus $69 million profit the prior year.

The Campeau family lost $450 million in less than one month's time. The children's fortunes plummeted from $30-40 million to $1.5-2.0 million each. Dunn and Bradstreet advised manufacturers to stop shipping merchandise to the Campeau stores, Allied and Federated.

It became the largest Chapter 11 filing in United States' retail history. At least 100,000 Allied and Federated employees were advised their jobs were protected under a Chapter 11 filing. The big money losers were First Boston, owed $525 million, Manufacturer's Trust, $145 million, Paine Webber, $96 million, and Dillard Reed, $48 million. First Boston had loaned money to Campeau to finance the Allied purchase also.

Campeau's actions had caused trouble in Canada. This was his second bankruptcy; he had also suffered a quarrel with the Catholic Church over a divorce and remarriage.

The New York Times of January 17, 1990, reported, "Any corporate executive can figure out how to file for bankruptcy when the bottom drops out of the business. It took the special genius of Robert Campeau, chairman of the Campeau Corporation, to figure out how to bankrupt more than 250 profitable department stores. The dramatic jolt to Bloomingdale's, Abraham Strauss, Jordan Marsh and the other profitable stores reflected his overreaching grasp and oversized ego."

Early leveraged buyouts, (LBO's), probably increased productivity, helping the economy. The recent LBO's benefited the target company's shareholders who received high takeover prices at the expense of bondholders, creditors and employees. When the government stops subsidizing such speculation with tax breaks, we will have less to worry about.

An outsider with no knowledge of retailing was the proverbial "bull in the china shop." Bloomingdales at its peak was devastated, as were I. Magnin and Bullock's when they became Macy stores. Bonwit Teller, a fine specialty store, didn't survive. Stores taken over by May Company survived but never reflected their former status.

George Herscu and Robert Campeau had more in common than their real estate developments. Both men were determined to have their way at any price.

A Romanian-born survivor of a Nazi labor camp, Herscu went to Australia in his twenties because he believed there was opportunity there. His first venture was a small bar similar to our convenience store. Not long afterwards, he and two partners set up Hersfield Developments, which became Australia's most successful developer of shopping centers. His timing was perfect.

In 1985, Herscu took control of Hooper Corporation, a fifty-eight-year-old Australian real estate company, that he felt was stodgy. The company was the largest publicly held real estate company in the country with $1 billion in assets and forty offices in Australia.

Earlier Hooper had moved to the United States where they developed more than 1400 houses in Atlanta in 1984.

Herscu, like Campeau saw great potential in the Unites States. The rags-to-riches gambler said he was inspired by Lee Iacocca's autobiography, which he had read several times. He started with buying fourteen Merrill Lynch offices with the idea of getting into Real Estate Investment Trusts, REITS. Next, he acquired a number of retail outlets in Australia and an eleven-store chain of jewelry stores in San Francisco.

While Campeau was talking of 100 regional malls anchored by his prestigious stores, Herscu was developing plans for seven Hooper Corporation Megamalls. Herscu said that Campeau picked up on his idea.

Herscu was looking for prestigious stores to anchor his mega-malls. New York accountants were looking for a white knight. Influenced by a change in the tax law, the Altman Foundation, which gave its earnings to New York charities each year, sold the venerable 5th Avenue store to B. A. Realty Associates for only $100 million in 1986. The Realty Associates then sold the chain, minus the real estate to two accountants backed by foreign money. The accountants were in over their heads and were bailed out by Hooper. Herscu first bought Bonwit Teller from Campeau, who was diverting some of his poorer performers from the Allied takeover. Then he picked up two Texas bankrupt stores—Sakowitz and Frost Brothers, and also the Parisian in Birmingham, Alabama.

After spending $380 million on stores, Herscu announced plans to build regional malls in Cincinnati, Denver, Atlanta and Tampa, with smaller malls in Raleigh, North Carolina, and Columbia, South Carolina.

Unlike Campeau, Herscu had not done his homework. Although he had gathered good names, only Parisian was a thriving operation. The morale of New York stores had hit a bottom, flooded with "for sale" signs.

As of March 1, 1989, Hooper had assets of $1.6 billion and liabilities of $1.4 billion. He offered assets for sale at unrealistic prices; suppliers cut off shipments of merchandise on August 1, 1989. B. Altman had not one piece of new fall merchandise. Ten days later Hooper Corporation filed for protection under Chapter 11. Although the store had lost its prestige, the doors had to be locked to control the crowds of bargain hunters and collectors of mementos of their favorite store.

Herscu tried to borrow money to no avail. Interest rates were twenty percent in Australia. Most of the properties were at bargain sale prices. Sakowitz went into bankruptcy. The Parisian was acquired by its former owner and is thriving today. Bonwit Teller and B. Altman's no longer exist as well as many lesser names.

George Herscu liked to think big, but was not well informed nor well focused. He was looking at megamalls, smaller malls, and a retail empire to anchor his malls, the housing market and downtown commercial buildings. At the same time, the United States was saturated with malls; he and Campeau looked at it as virgin territory.

Back in Australia, Herscu pleaded guilty to making secret payments to building officials in 1983. Sixty banks and 13,000 stockholders were caught in the squeeze. He was sentenced to five years for convicted bribery.

In three years, Herscu had transformed a conservative company with a secure future into an aggressive retail and property giant with the hope of fantastic profits. A former Hooper director described him as "a fast train that, confronted with an obstacle, would run off the track." Unfortunately, Campeau and Herscu, with the help of May Co.'s destruction of Lord & Taylor, changed forever the retail scene on 5th Avenue.

When I first knew New York City, 34th Street to 42nd Street was filled with interesting stores on both sides of 5th Avenue with the exception of the New York City library. The upper portion of 5th Avenue today boasts only two fine stores—Saks Fifth Avenue and Bergdorf Goodman. The former 1950s fine

233

department stores and specialty stores at their summit, remind us that Fifth Avenue was once the world's fashion street.

Emily, the poor are thankful for what they have and the rich want more.

Love,

Laurie

Chapter Three

Changing Demographics Change Stores

 Dear Emily,

Does it all make sense now? So what really happened to a fine institution, born in Europe, perfected in America, and all but extinct in little more than one century? There is no simple answer.

The arrival of the automobile brought the customer to town. Twenty-five years later, the automobile made suburban life attractive. Soon a few stores created a shopping center or a strip center near the customer. The shopping center paved the way for the mall.

Department stores were losing downtown traffic to the shopping centers when the store principals decided that their future role was to anchor large suburban malls. Soon, large cities had at least one mall, and many had several. Often, three to four department stores became anchor stores in lively malls in many cities.

Unquestionably, the success of the malls led to the deterioration of the expansive and the expensive downtown stores that offered wide assortments and unbelievable service. No one wanted to see them disappear, but, economically, they were no longer feasible. Those that did survive had to make major adjustments.

Aggressive real estate developers found new sites and department store owners signed on. Exorbitant interest rates put the brakes on the expansion in the 1980s, or we could have been even more overbuilt than we are now.

There are roughly 1500 malls in the United States, but the love affair has ended. Closings are being announced. April 16, 2009, General Growth, the nation's second largest owner of shopping malls, filed for Chapter 11 to restructure its $27 billion deal. If shopping dollars decrease and shopping patterns change, what will happen to all the expensive real estate?

Competition for retail dollars continues to increase. Internet, EBay, and the proliferation of catalogues have carved out a slice of the retail dollars. The love affair with technology has claimed many of the customer's allowances for clothing.

With China being the epicenter of all classifications of merchandise in all price lines, it is more difficult for department stores to distinguish themselves from each other and the discounters. Walmart and Target have been blamed for the changed retail scene. Mom and Pop stores, the local hardware store, the pharmacy and the local grocer have all but disappeared. The customers who loved the stimulation and excitement of shopping in a fine store do not relate to the confusion of the discounters, but that segment of the population is disappearing. Today's shopper doesn't often expect quality, good taste and service. Discounters have made available to the masses goods that otherwise would not have been accessible. The taste level in Target stores, however, seems to be higher than the other discounters. Perhaps this is due to their Dayton-Hudson department store roots.

Allocation of space in the stores has changed along with the demographics. When I was a buyer at Ivey's, women's size clothing was relegated to the back wall— volume was light. Today, large sizes dominate quality locations and are huge gross margin producers. Have you noticed all the oversized furniture featured by furniture stores? Queen or King-sized mattresses and bedding make full-size obsolete. Shoes come only in medium and large widths in department stores. What do people with narrow feet do? Who needs five-finger gloves (no thumbs) and square-toe socks?

The suburbs and accompanying casual lifestyle have supported the overwhelming growth of sportswear for the entire family. Some of that growth has transferred from dresses, coat and suit departments. Now, the French Salon had little or no space in the malls. The Chinese do a better job executing sportswear than they do other classifications. Well-tailored fashion coats have also been replaced by weather coats due to lack of quality tailoring overseas.

The lifestyle change is also reflected in the home store and the bridal registry. Silver plate and pewter have replaced sterling; casual dinnerware has replaced fine china; sturdy glassware outsells fine crystal; fine linens have been ousted by casual linens.

Have current lifestyle changes made the fine department stores dinosaurs? Has greed on Wall Street affected the standard of living for the masses? On the other hand, maybe the consciousness of the public is moving from a "me" to a "we" attitude. Maybe public service will replace private possessions. Maybe lavish lifestyles will be less acceptable.

"Live simply so more people may simply live."—
Gandhi.

The exorbitant interest rates of the 1980s, the advancement of technology, the competition from the discounters, the internet, catalogues, and world trade foretold a changing retail scene. The fine stores should have been allowed to plan their own exits—not to be murdered by four greedy, strong-minded, misinformed men with immeasurable egos. Only the bankers did worse when the CEO's acted like gods and left the ruins to be rescued by the taxpayers.

The retail shuffle was the first large disruption of an industry effecting millions of employees and customers. The dishevelment of Federated took place in the late 1980s and the stores have been slowly recovering. Retailing in the United States reached its peak in the late 1970s, early 1980s and likely will not attain its former glory.

Emily, it doesn't bode well that the department stores were the first victims of the take-over upheaval. Big aims to be biggest.

Love,

Lauren

Chapter Four

Merchants Contribute to Own Failure—Loss of Credibility

Dear Emily,

I would love to think that all the above circumstances have accounted for the despicable status of the department store today. I would be remiss if I didn't mention the merchant's contribution to the fall and lack of recovery twenty years later.

In the 1950s, a fine department store sold at least seventy-five percent of its merchandise at regular prices as opposed to fifteen percent today. Markdowns were taken after Christmas and announced in a one-page ad. Today this sale, supported by specially bought merchandise along with after-Thanksgiving sales are the largest sales days of the year.

At Ivey's, we only bought merchandise specifically for a sale for the Anniversary sale every May and again for the Harvest sale in the fall. We would select one or two best selling items from stock in each department and ask the manufacturer to sell us enough for a three-day sale. If necessary, we would take a lower mark-on and offer it as a great buy. Our aim was to sell every piece and, if we had made a good choice, we did. Loyal customers looked forward to these quality events. Markdowns were used to move end-of-season merchandise.

Somewhere along the way greed set in, and merchants started buying into the events in volume. The events expanded to after Easter, July Fourth Sale, Harvest Sales joined after Thanksgiving and after-Christmas Sales. Technology has made possible sale pricing without red-penciling. Today every weekend carries a sale. Monday is apt to start the week with a sale. The customer has been trained to avoid paying regular price for anything. The stores have lost their credibility with their customers.

Unlike former days, when stores were run by the family of the founder, today most decisions are made by outsiders. These hired CEO's and merchandise managers have limited short-term visions, not concerned with the long-term benefit of the institution. How can credibility be reclaimed?

The stores have contributed to the mess by offering so much private label merchandise carrying exorbitant built-in markdown dollars. With advertising rates rising, how do drug stores run tabloids every week without built in markups?

Clothing made in China carries an unusually high mark-up. Liz Claiborne and Jones of New York have jeopardized their franchises and tarnished their names by offering cheaply made merchandise of poor fabrics at ridiculous retails. The customer is smarter than they credit. One finds as much of these two labels in discounters as in the department stores. How long can this last?

Today's pricing reflects what the traffic will bear— not the intrinsic value. Manufacturers moved offshore for cheap wages—not better product. The largest profits are often made by the middleman and the retailers. Wages are still low in China; their wealth comes from the number of workers. Quality control has given way to quantity. When the public tires of the rip-off, some smart entrepreneurs are going to find they can reclaim some classes of merchandise and show the public how "made in America" compares with "made in China."

Where are the designers on 7th Avenue and Europe getting their inspiration? Diana Vreelands' outstanding shows involving the Fashion Institute and the Metropolitan Museum in the 1970s were an inspiration for all 7th Avenue. Today, accessories: handbags, scarves and shoes have stolen the show.

Emily, I am delighted that I lived in the Golden Age of the fine stores and enjoyed the good taste, civility, creativity, superb service and the civic support of the owners.

Love,

Lauren

Chapter Five

Greed Takes Over Financials

Dear Emily,

After moving back to Winston-Salem, I was an observer of several more examples of greed. Paul Sticht, a former president of Federated Stores, had served on the Reynolds Industries board for several years before he retired. He was a familiar face at A.M.C. meetings, and I had visited Federated headquarters in Columbus, Ohio. A Lazarus executive said that Sticht held up the company for the largest retirement package Federated had ever awarded. When asked what he planned to do in his retirement, he answered management that he planned to spend the rest of his life as a philanthropist. He had already accepted a position with Reynolds as President and Chief Operating Officer, while bargaining with Federated. Soon he became CEO and Chairman. At Reynolds, he expanded the company, but the stock suffered. Sticht and a former banker from Charlotte unsuccessfully attempted a buyout. This unsuccessful move put the company into action.

According to *Barbarians at the Gate*, When

Kohlberg-Kravis won the bid, the new president wanted to move its headquarters to Atlanta. The board was split, so Paul Sticht was called back from retirement to break a hung vote. Sticht cut a deal. He would vote for the Atlanta move, but only if the president, James Johnston, agreed that Reynolds would build a Sticht Rehabilitation Center for the Wake Forest University Hospital.

It is a state-of-the-art building, but years later, less than half the building is used for the purpose intended. Seems there is a lack of funds to support the project. Could it be that the philanthropist forgot to endow his namesake? A $6 million facility should have deserved a substantial endowment. Could it have been greed? No remorse for the city he called home and that launched his late success?

When I moved into the village of Old Salem in the late 1950s, there was a most unusual food shop that appealed to the girls at nearby Salem College. Mr. Vernon Rudolph, a World War II veteran, had concocted a yeast doughnut that was a delicious, light sweet and was well accepted as Krispy Kreme. It was a large, private, successful business during his life. His widow sold it to Beatrice Foods, who, after a few years, found it was not a good fit with its conglomerate. It was picked up by an investment group that had visions for going international. The brand had never been promoted, and the new owners laid out an ambitious approach. Success bred success, but the management lost its head when they failed to cut back while the war on sweets was worldwide. Business was falling while expenses were rising. The three top officers padded the quarterly reports for several years—protecting their jobs and bonuses. Recently the three were ordered by the SEC to return much of the added bonuses. Greed!

We thought greed had reached its pinnacle early in 2008, but it had only paused for an unprecedented, calculated and accelerated attack.

Emily, after watching the demise of the department stores, I've been sickened by how many families have been hurt by the banking institutions. It seems to be another case of big business taking advantage of the little guy.

First Union Bank, located in Charlotte, North Carolina, had been on a wild acquisition spree that had damaged its name as well as its financial strength; meanwhile, Bud Baker, president of Wachovia, was observing from the sidelines. Neither bank was enjoying good health in 2008 when SunTrust of Atlanta made an unsolicited bid for Wachovia. In hindsight, Wachovia shareholders would have fared well with a positive vote. Instead, management and shareholders hastily approved a merger with First Union, which was in need of a more prestigious name as well as resources. Bud Baker readily accepted his reward–a $14 million bonus plus $1 million each year for life.

Ken Thompson of First Union assumed the new presidency and from 2003-07 made wild purchases that moved the new Wachovia from sixth place in volume to the fourth-largest national bank. His unsound decision to pay $25.3 billion for West Financial Company, burdened with baggage of heavy loans, was his last large mistake. Fees were increased on customers who could least afford them. Employees were told that there was no money for increases the same week the paper carried an article that Ken Thompson had been awarded an $8 million bonus.

The bank made unqualified loans, packaged them and sold them to mortgage companies for a profit. With only a few remaining days until the bankruptcy would be declared, Citigroup offered $1 per share with the government's backing. Wells Fargo stepped up and made a $7 offer. After much discussion about legality, the voices of outraged stockholders were heard and the sale went to the highest bidder.

Employees, retirees, and stockholders were devastated. Millions, maybe billions, were lost due to irresponsible decisions made by unqualified leaders and boards. How can they sleep nights knowing many workers lost their life savings? Needed are bankers with compassion for the masses that supported them. To date, no Wall-Streeter or banker has been investigated.

The housing disaster at this time is far from over; many foreclosures are being questioned. Under Thompson's tenure, $376 billion in illegal drug money from Mexico was laundered. In 2010, the president of Wells Fargo was paid $21 million versus the $7 million the prior year due to the successful acquisition of Wachovia.

After following the phenomenal success of the discount broker, I wonder why we cannot have discount banks. Schwab offers more timely facts and more efficient service than most full-service brokers do and at a fraction of the cost.

In most cities, banks occupy the finest buildings in the town and the banker is the highest-paid executive. Do banks need ivory towers and top-paid executives when the supporting clients are ignored?

After the Great Depression of the 1930s, the government promised that measures had been taken that would prevent the disaster from occurring again. Instead, the present depression was caused by the same government including Freddie Mac, Fannie Mae, and the Washington decision that all Americans should own a home regardless of qualifications. The bigger the bank, the bigger the greed and the greater the fall! The customers, stockholders, and the taxpayers shall pay for their folly for years to come.

Increased fees and outrageous interest on charge cards speak of the banks attitude to its base customer. This customer would welcome a smaller, kinder bank that offers more economical banking. Credit Unions are thriving. Locations in an unused or historical building and hiring an experienced banker with good common sense would be a plus. There are capable young men and women who would welcome a job that pays thousands, not millions. These banks should target their customers who require less service and leave the large accounts to the full-line banks.

Presently, the large banks are the least-respected and trusted of any large institutions. They have blown their chances to correct their course. There are enough unsatisfied customers to demand and get changes.

More than a year has passed and the financial sector seems not to have learned anything from the 2008 disaster. Salaries and bonuses remain exorbitant. In October 2009, Washington announced that new laws would protect the public from further greed from the banks. Immediately Wells Fargo and Bank of America announced increases in fees and in some instances as much as doubled interest rates on current charge cards. The banks moved overnight; the government said they could not prepare for the change until January. The bill became obsolete. Few banks that received free taxpayer money showed their appreciation and credibility.

The last red flag is that many of the largest banks are being investigated for making questionable foreclosures. A temporary freeze on foreclosures has been issued. The too-big-to-fail banks continue to show their true colors.

How could the world's youngest nation lose its way so soon? Because we are so powerful, our fall has affected the entire world. The "Greatest Generation" has been followed by the "Greediest Generation."

Not all of our problems are systemic. With lack of confidence in our government, we are looking for leaders with integrity, honesty, character, compassion, respect and good common sense. The "Me Generation" politicians put themselves above the welfare of their constituents.

To date, no female banker, or female Wall-Streeter has been challenged by the public. Maybe it is time to give more deserving women opportunities. The "Big Boys Clubs" have blown it. Alan Greenspan disappointed the public when he said that he failed to predict the recession because there was no model. What happened to "thinking outside the box?"

The history of the twentieth century American department stores chronicles the social history of the young nation. The Robber Baron Era highly contributed to the growth of the finest stores. With competition limited to their few peers, the stores went all out to please the discerning customer. The Sherman Trust Act of 1890 was the vehicle used to curtail big business but not before the Astors, Carnegies, Fuchs, Rockefellers, and others left huge endowments we are benefitting from even today.

The First World War, followed by the Great Depression and World War II allowed for survival of the department store, although with little growth except for home-related merchandise. By the mid 1960s, the world was on the way to visible recovery and soon healthy growth in the stores was unlike anything before.

Greed motivated mall developers to overbuild. Merchants had little choice but to go along. Four men with few qualifications wanted to make their mark in the retail world and played havoc with an industry and millions of lives. My thought is it attracted these "visionaries" because it was where the greatest growth had been and they felt they deserved their share. Despite the failure of these men, other questionable and brazen attempts to "get their share" followed. Our present, prolonged recession is the result of greed in all areas of business from charitable to government to private to publicly held companies.

Emily, let's hope that greed has finally peaked. Americans have so much to be grateful for that now is the time to show it.

Love,

Laurie

Chapter Six

Status of the Museums—Peer Tastemakers

Dear Emily,

Meanwhile the American museum, which arrived on the scene simultaneously with the American department store, progressed slowly. Not until the 1950s when the Metropolitan Museum purchased the Rembrandt masterpiece: *Aristotle Contemplating the Bust of Homer* for $2 million did the museum enter into a period of dramatic growth.

The decline of the central city and the huge department stores caused more interest to shift to the museums as sources of enlightenment. Not since the decline of the Fortnight in the better department stores, has there been competition with the museum for public influence.

Diana Vreeland's costume shows at the Metropolitan were a notable influence on fashion and included: The World of Balenciaga, 1973; The Glory of Russian Costume, 1976-77; Fashion of the Hapsburg Era, Austria-Hungary, 1979-80; Yves St. Laurent, Twenty-Five Years of Design, 1983-84; and Man and the Horse, 1984-85.

Emily, the riding habit worn by Ellen Glasgow, the antebellum writer from Richmond was featured at the Man and the Horse show. You would have loved to see that!

Any meaningful influence is sadly lacking today. Since St. Johns Knits have gone "trashy," and many of the designers are imitating Aileen Fisher, Lily Pulitzer with her quality fabrics and superb workmanship is enjoying a revival in the South that surpasses her original lines in the 1970s. Americans want quality!

Although museums are not-for-profit institutions, they are not insulated from the ripples of the economy. Their biggest problem comes from Washington where Congress loves to tweak the tax laws, often having a dramatic effect on donations. The Tax Reform of 1986 reduced benefits for donating appreciated property and donations declined 32.8% from 1986-89. This led to an upheaval in many museums when directors and boards reappraised their collections. Some museums sold quality works to fill a void in contemporary art. This in turn upset many donors.

Escalating costs have accounted for fewer major shows at large museums, but there is no longer a contest for where the public finds its cultural centers. Transportation costs have caused attendance to drop in regional museums but most urban museums continue to thrive, stimulating and educating the public taste.

Love,

Laurie

Conclusion

 Dear Emily,

If I were asked to do a five-year prediction, as when I worked, I would have difficulty. I can see more people returning to downtown living, which would support more Mom and Pop stores, but I fail to see the return of the fine department store. If department stores can no longer provide service by few, if any, salespeople, knowledge of product, good assortments, quality merchandise, and if it continues to sell the majority of its stock off-price, what is to differentiate it from the discounter? The specialty stores will expand and do well as they pamper the customers and provide better merchandise.

The most encouraging message pertaining to the future of the American department store comes from a recent CNN financial report. An official from Macy's said that in the fall of 2009, the company had launched a "My Macy's" program in ten large cities including Chicago and Detroit. Here a percentage of the stocks were geared to the distinct demographics of the customer. Since the trial was launched, the company enjoyed a 2.5% increase in the targeted stores over the total corporate sales. With the success of the program, the project continues to expand. I would like to see them return the Marshall Field's sign and clock in Chicago and the Dayton-Hudson sign in Detroit.

Marshall Field's could be another Bloomingdales. Dayton-Hudson deserves a break. I feel he could see two happy, proud cities repay Macy's generously.

"For everything there is a season, and a time for every matter under the sun"
                                        Ecclesiastes 3:1

Emily, our lives are highly influenced by when and where we were born and who our parents were, over which we have no control. My parents were victims of the Great Depression. They never enjoyed the comforts of their parents—no fault of theirs—but they were the salt of the earth, honest, kind, tenacious and loving. My Granddaddy Smith sent eight out of nine of his surviving children to the academy and/or to college. My parents wanted their children to enjoy a better life than they had and they set an excellent example of frugality.

When I returned from New York, I lived at home for several years. Dad suggested that since I had no expenses I should save every other paycheck. With obligations only for gas, parking, lunch and clothes, I thought this a good idea.

I found no problem saving half of what I brought home and continued to do that for my working career. I never felt deprived. Later I was provided a company car and other benefits that helped the budget.

When Mr. Ivey sent me to a Dale Carnegie Lecture, my father was anxious to hear the advice. Carnegie's number one admonishment was always to dress better than one could afford. Good dressing and immaculate grooming promotes confidence. Dad immediately said that Mr. Ivey would have done well to have saved his money. Actually, Dad thought it was a good idea for all business people to be well dressed.

My entire career was influenced by events over which I had absolutely no control. This included The Great Depression, World War II, new interest in American fashion, the move to the suburbs, a more casual lifestyle, and then the arrival of the mall. I tried to concentrate on those things I could control—taste and timing. Personal taste is cultivated through exposure but timing must be learned. My General Merchandising Manager at Ivey's taught me my best lesson—timing—the correct balance between current and forward merchandise. For a fashion department, he advised at least thirty percent be forward stock at the height of the season. This allowed for developing trends and best sellers before the new season. It also cut back on markdowns. If Dillards could have adapted this theory, they could have owned the moderate-to-better fashion business. Their taste level is great, but too much valuable floor space is allocated to obsolete stock. The age of the stock reflects the health of a store.

Not until Washington understands the importance that small businesses and small banks play in our economy will we see a return to prosperity. Small and medium-sized banks say that paperwork prevents their return to profitability. Tax breaks given to companies going offshore are a disgrace. Ex-president Clinton, who encouraged the lowering of tariffs on textiles, now says it is time to return some manufacturing jobs to America. We have the best work ethics—if challenged, only by the Germans. With the cost of fuel escalating, why should we pay more for the transportation of large appliances than the product cost to produce—not to mention the quality and repairs. A well-known men's shirt manufacturer recently opened a large factory in Eastern North Carolina. Rather than spend all our emphasis on exports, we could cut back on imports to help balance the budget. Not all of the unemployed people are candidates for technology jobs. Small businesses could create many jobs, return pride and a purpose to many lives as they work with their hands.

When we reclaim our Gross National Product, make more products in America, we can order less, reorder more and have more interesting, better quality assortments in our stores again.

"Give the customer what she wants," not "give her what we want her to have" would be the greatest approach the department store could adopt. Marshall Field, John Wanamaker, the Rich family, J. B. Ivey, the Thalhimer Brothers all made their marks by making every effort to please their loyal customers. Human nature has not changed—stores have. Nothing woos the customer like a little special attention. May Macy's approach spread and save the remnants of the once-glorious department store.

Emily, I have been blessed to live in the time of the "Great Churches," the "Greatest Generation," the "Grand Emporiums," with civility, character, honest work and respect. Changes are needed today, not just for the sake of change. When it contributes to the best for the most people, honestly and unselfishly, confidence will then return.

To quote Sir Winston Churchill, "We make a living by what we earn. We make a life by what we give."

Love,

Laura

P.S. Emily, I hope you have enjoyed my ramblings as much as I enjoyed recalling them.

Acknowledgements

Although retailing would not have been their choice, members of my family always supported my efforts. In the 1940s, a woman was expected to be a teacher, a nurse or a secretary. My choice was not conventional.

Eighteen months living in New York City was responsible for developing my taste by exposure to all the museums and to the world's best specialty and department stores.

Lord & Taylor was the best possible training ground and gave me the desire and confidence to pursue a career in this exciting field. The well-dressed women buyers at Lord & Taylor came on the floor occasionally, beautifully groomed and always wearing a hat. (This prevented them from being approached by the customers when they couldn't serve them). How I aspired to the exciting life of a fashion buyer!

My friends in New York prevented me from having idle time and enriched my life by introducing me to all the landmarks and interesting events.

In Charlotte, I was given the opportunity to test my wings by the management at Ivey's. It was Mr. George Ivey Jr. who launched my career, and to whom I am grateful, and he also influenced my move to a company that accepted the equality of women and men.

My move to Winston-Salem was a big gamble, but luckily, the timing was perfect. I accepted an undefined job description; it would become what we made of it—sink or swim.

I wish to express my thanks to Sherwood Michael, Charles Thalhimer and Evelyn Sosnik (deceased) for their unending support. Also, my thanks to all the loyal employees for their dedicated support to make the new undertaking work and to produce better results than we had anticipated.

I am appreciative of all the opportunities the Thalhimer organization afforded me: those A.M.C. meetings when I was the only female, my first trip to California, the many trips to A.M.C. stores all over the country. These trips gave me insights into other cities and sister stores. Their operations helped influence me in our position and our store's potential.

The many month-long spring trips to Europe proved to be my best education. The world's finest museums, performing arts, cathedrals, churches, the finest hotels and restaurants gave me an appreciation for the history and culture of others. I developed, and still have, great respect and compassion for those who gave so much during World War I and World War II.

We were in Europe for many Easter weekends and joined the masses in Rome to see and hear Pope John Paul II address the throngs. One Easter Sunday, I attended services at Westminster Abbey in London, but my first memory is of freezing in that handsome massive structure with no heat. The reading of the scripture was beautiful as only an Englishmen can enunciate.

My trips to the Orient introduced me to a culture that was new and different. I still have apprehension that we gave them all our textile business when Congress lowered the tariff too much too soon. It was as if we opened the floodgates. We exchanged quality for quantity and are still paying.

I wish to acknowledge and thank all the men and women with the resources that supported us so loyally; to the management and personnel of A.M.C.—the "Big League" of buying offices. Their coverage of domestic and foreign markets and timely reports made our job more productive. Their collecting, coordination, and presentation of overseas merchandise, whether in San Francisco, Europe or the Orient, was a fete accompli.

My thanks to the editors who agreed to read my thesis and suggested that I write it in first person. Also to Mr. Stanley Marcus who read the thesis and referred me to his publisher who agreed with the other editors.

Thanks to many friends who encouraged me during the slow process.

My appreciation to an anonymous consultant whose fresh ideas were valuable.

I am indebted to Dr. Frank and Bea Levin, Susan Meny without whose contribution this would not exist.

I would be remiss if I didn't acknowledge my many loyal friends who have contributed to an exciting, stimulating retirement: Charlie and Nancy Thomas, Erma Adkins, Sylvia Alderson, Dick and Peggy Ayscue, Helen and Allen Blackford, Pat and Sam Blythe, Betsy and Neil Clark, , Agnes Canzona, Carol Crumley, Kitty Felts, Geneva Ford, Joe Floyd, Brian Haislip, Lynette and Robert Harrell, Mildred Helms, Joyce and Barry Kingman (deceased), Evelyn Lukeman, Sarah McFarland, Julie Mackie, Marion Mctyre, Martha Moore, Betsy and Walt Nading, Ann and Tom Pierce, Sue and Kenneth Phillips, Sarah and Allen Rohrbough (deceased), Olivia Sharp, Margaret Snow (deceased), Phil Saylor, Jeannette Simmons, Eugene Simmons, Nancy and Jerry Warren, Nancy and Harry Underwood, Jack and Sylvia Yarborough, and Ervin Schiff (deceased).

To: Centenary United Methodist Church, its embracing congregation, its outstanding ministering staff, inspiring music, and expansive educational program.

I am highly indebted to my dear friend Emily Lawrence for contributing to the exciting career I enjoyed. She influenced my bold move to New York and then made sure I met her friends and discovered the city. Our interest in fashion was just one area New York encouraged. Also, we enjoyed the museums, churches, concerts and the stimulating atmosphere of New York during our 18 months of diligent exploring. We remained good friends via the telephone. I so miss her.

To: One who made possible a long, fascinating, grateful life.

Love,

Laurie

Emily Southall Lawrence
July 12, 1915 ~ August 16, 2010

Emily Lawrence was born in Murfreesboro, North Carolina where she lived until she graduated from Chowan College. She taught school before moving to join NACA at Langley Field, Virginia. She attended an interior school of design in New York City before working for Eastern Airlines. After getting her Masters in Library Science at the University of North Carolina, Chapel Hill, she worked as Children's Librarian at the Richmond Public Library.

8250908R0

Made in the USA
Charleston, SC
22 May 2011